301.361
WAL

THE CHICKENBONE SPECIAL

COLLEGE FOR HUMAN SERVICES
LIBRARY
345 HUDSON STREET
NEW YORK, N.Y. 10014

DWAYNE E. WALLS

The Chickenbone Special

Harcourt Brace Jovanovich, Inc. New York

Copyright © 1970, 1971 by Dwayne E. Walls
All rights reserved. No part of this publication may be reproduced or transmitted in any form or by any means, electronic or mechanical, including photocopy, recording, or any information storage and retrieval system, without permission in writing from the publisher.

ISBN 0-15-117160-2
Library of Congress Catalog Card Number: 70-142099
Printed in the United States of America

B C D E

CONTENTS

Preface   vii

Introduction   xv

1   Taking a Ride   3
2   Let New York Be Like I Think It Is   8
3   Heaven, Hell and Baltimore   18
4   The Last Crop   30
5   A Woman Blessed   39
6   The Golden Token   44
7   The Station   61
8   Cream of the Crop   66
9   A Busy Day   72
10 The Chickenbone Special   77
11 The Fantastic Four   87
12 Window Seat   102
13 New York Is All Right   117
14 Good-by, Mayflower   126
15 Willie Durham's House   141

Contents

16 The Great Migration 152
17 The Wanderers 157
18 Rochester 167
19 The Fantastic Two 171
20 Fort Greene 178
21 Home Again 189
22 Georgia Mae Takes a Ride 199
23 A Matter of Pride 205
24 The Crop and the Draft 215
25 Home Is Not Home Any More 219
26 Thanksgiving 223

Epilogue 228

PREFACE

Although the nation's rural-to-urban migration has been written about extensively during the past two or three decades, the subject remains largely unfamiliar to most Americans. One reason for this, in my judgment, is that the countless books on the subject have been produced mainly by sociologists, anthropologists and demographers for the benefit of other sociologists, anthropologists and demographers. This is not to say, or even to imply, that those books do not have merit. Many are excellent, and almost all of them represent a great deal of hard work. If they have no appeal to readers outside the professional and academic spheres, the reason no doubt is because they never were intended to appeal to nonprofessional, nonacademic audiences.

I began this book keenly aware of my own limitations and more than a little doubtful that I could offer any worthwhile contribution to the body of knowledge already existing on the subject. I knew that I was not equipped by training or inclination to produce a scholarly work. I had no desire to write a book merely to be able then to say that I had written a book. Nonetheless, I *did* want to write a book—not any book, but this particular book.

My interest in migration goes back to 1962 when,

with another reporter, I wrote a series of articles for the Charlotte *Observer* on election fraud in the mountains of North Carolina. We were able to prove conclusively that mountain politicians were routinely stealing elections with the use of absentee ballots. In the course of the investigation, I was appalled to discover the number of legitimate absentee ballots that were cast every year in mountain counties because of the heavy out-migration that had begun years earlier. (In a sense, my interest had already been kindled because I am one product of out-migration. My parents left the mountains as newlyweds and wandered throughout the Piedmont section of North Carolina for years before settling down.) After the election-fraud series had run, I reorganized my file to build a new one on migration. Later, I did occasional stories on migration and, in 1968, collaborated with another reporter—James K. Batten, who was then in the *Observer*'s Washington bureau—to produce a series of articles on rural poverty and migration. This series coincided with the publication of a report by the President's National Advisory Commission on Rural Poverty, which dealt exhaustively with the problems of migration.

After publication of that series, Batten and I discussed expanding it into a book. We were not able to write the book, but the editors at the *Observer* agreed that migration was a story worth sticking to. So I began attending conferences and seminars on the subject, meanwhile writing some follow-up stories. One of those stories led me by accident to the discovery of the "Chickenbone Special." I rode the train North in June

Preface

of 1968, and it was then that I knew I had to write the book.

Several weeks before I first rode the train, I had heard Dr. C. E. Bishop (now chancellor of the University of Maryland) describe the nation's rural-to-urban migration as the greatest movement of human beings in history. Aboard the train, I realized fully for the first time, I think, that the migrants were significant beyond the fact of their numbers. These people were not moving solely to find greater opportunity, as my parents had; as hundreds of thousands have done, and as tens of thousands continue doing every year in this country. The important thing about this migration, I determined, was that it was an *unwilling* migration. Human beings were moving not because they *wanted* to move but because they *had* to move.

I wanted to write about these people in human terms that other people would understand and appreciate. I wanted to popularize the subject of migration, and I knew that the book would have to be readable, above all else, if it were to be worth the effort. Yet it also had to be believable; and to be believable, it had to be absolutely factual.

I decided that to keep the work manageable, I would try to dramatize the migration of the many in a simple, narrative account of a few. Carrying a tape recorder and several dozen tapes, I moved into the little black community of Mayflower in May of 1969 to begin the search for the few. I wanted to live as closely as possible to the people I intended to write about, and so I accepted the hospitality of Mr. and Mrs. Ernest Turner, the one family in the community that had room for me without upsetting the family life. I lived with the Turners for a month, meantime traveling back and forth between Warren County, North Carolina, and Williamsburg County, South Carolina, interviewing potential outmigrants. Those finally selected for intensive work and inclusion in the book (out of several dozen initial interviews) were selected for a number of reasons. They had to be willing subjects first of all—willing to allow me to intrude into their lives, to ask questions that seemed at times to be unending and sometimes very personal; willing to allow me to travel with them and badger them again and again in follow-up interviews. They had to be fairly representative of one or another group in the reasons for their leaving. Partly, too, it was a matter of convenience and scheduling for me.

My one salute to scientific method was a self-imposed restriction. I insisted on talking only with those persons who already had made a decision to migrate, because I did not want my presence to influence them. I also tried not to influence them during travel and on arrival in the urban areas, but I cannot say with any certainty whether I succeeded or failed.

Some readers might wonder how I came to know the conversations and states of mind attributed to persons in the narrative. The answer is that I was present in many cases. In others, I reconstructed events and thoughts with detailed, sometimes painful questioning. The success of this technique is attributable less to the questioner than to the continued willingness of the questioned to respond. I did not actually hear Donnie Gibson say his prayer two nights before he left home.

Preface

He told me about it and reconstructed it for me on the train headed North, during a long talk about his religious beliefs. Follow-up interviews with all of the principal subjects in the book continued into December of 1969. One can learn a great deal about almost anything or anyone in seven months of constant questioning.

The fruit of all the questions might be called a nonfiction novel. But I must emphasize here that nothing in the manuscript is conjecture. The words, the thoughts, the feelings ascribed to all individuals mentioned in the book are *their* words, *their* thoughts, *their* feelings. They exist on my tapes and, in some cases of description and detail, in my note pads.

The names are real names, with the exceptions of Donnie Gibson's three sisters in Brooklyn, who asked to remain anonymous.

I have tried in this book to use simple language to tell a simple story about a national problem that is anything but simple. I hope the work has some merit.

DWAYNE E. WALLS

Charlotte, N.C.

ACKNOWLEDGMENTS

This book is the product of more than the one man who did the writing. It was conceived in the spring of 1968, when I collaborated with James K. Batten, on a series of articles on rural poverty and migration. Jim Batten could not join me in producing the book. But I must acknowledge that the idea was as much his as mine, and I do so gladly and gratefully.

I am indebted also to a number of other people and organizations who contributed measurably to the year's work: Dr. Raymond M. Wheeler and Paul Anthony of the Southern Regional Council; Carey McWilliams of the *Nation* magazine; George H. Esser, Jr., of the Ford Foundation; Dr. Norman W. Schul of the University of North Carolina at Charlotte; Donald G. Tacheron, Dr. Evron M. Kirkpatrick and Dr. Howard R. Penniman of the American Political Science Association.

Grants to support the research, travel and writing were provided by the American Political Science Association, the Ford Foundation, the Louis M. Rabinowitz Foundation, the Southern Regional Council and my employer, the Charlotte *Observer*. I am indebted to each of these organizations. But I am especially grateful for the encouragement of those persons who pleaded my

Acknowledgments

cause with the organizations and for their faith in my ability to produce a worthwhile book.

To Paul Anthony, who functioned throughout as a kind of gifted midwife; to Mrs. Diana Lee, who volunteered as secretary and typist and sometimes fretted as if it were *her* book; and to my wife, Judy, who felt at times as if she were living with a caged animal—to these a simple "thank you" somehow does not seem enough.

Finally, I must publicly acknowledge the greatest contribution of all—that of the people whose experiences are related in the book. Their contribution was their willingness to allow me to intrude into their lives and their minds; to live with them, to travel with them, to share in their most private fears and hopes. The story is their story. The words and the thoughts are their words and their thoughts, given generously and in simple faith that the gift would be used justly and that it might have some meaning.

To them I dedicate this book.

INTRODUCTION by Robert Coles

I don't suppose the author of this book is in line for any professorships. No universities are knocking on his door in an effort to obtain his time and energy. No sociologists or anthropologists or psychologists are asking for his help. He has not been made a professor of journalism. Nor can I imagine the great and wise federal government seeking Mr. Walls as a "consultant." For that matter the foundations, presumably more "flexible" or "imaginative," would also be unlikely candidates for the man's services. In an age of experts, he is a mere reporter. In an age preoccupied with statistics, he offers only the literate sentence composed by the sensible mind. And at a moment when just about everyone is taking up a "position," asserting a particular side of some argument, Mr. Walls offers us only life's sadness and humor, so mixed together that any self-respecting ideologue can only shudder at the devilish naïveté yet another Southern "small-town boy" has come up with—and has the nerve to think the rest of us might want to read and find significant.

I do not believe I have just belabored some unnecessary points. Nor am I being coy—though bitter, yes, and maybe a touch envious. For well over a decade I have worked with people very much like the ones Mr.

Introduction

Walls brings alive (that is what he does) in the following pages. For well over a decade I have done as he has done; I have gone to the cabins, sat and listened, felt embarrassed, felt like a damn fool, tried to get talk going, tried to learn things—grab on them, sort them out, put them down on paper. But I have come to those Southern cabins, gone with families on those buses and trains that pull out of Atlanta or Memphis or Birmingham, as a New Englander and a doctor—and also as a psychiatrist trained far too long at making diagnoses, taking note of "problems," fitting people into various categories, labeling them with an array of words. So equipped, I have done my work; "cultural disadvantage" certainly has not been *my* problem. In fact, if the particular men, women and children I now meet "out in the field" defy my wish to pin them down; if they undo my cool, reserved, clinical "face"; and if they make me stop and wonder, make me confused, make me a little envious of them as well as of Mr. Walls—then clearly I know enough to realize that I have been getting myself into a lot of trouble, and had best seek "help" of some kind, maybe from a social scientist who knows his "methodology," and maybe also from a good, tough psychiatrist who can spot in a flash someone "overinvolved" and "overidentified" and all the rest.

Again I must insist that I am not beating a dead horse. If only some of the murky-minded, evasive and even deceitful words that pass for "scholarship" were more obviously suspect or discredited. If only the universities really were less subject to the arbitrary and snobbish dictates of what some call "academic tradition." If only government officials (including legislators) and foundation executives did have the will and the courage to face the blunt and aching truths that a book like this presents—rather than hiding behind the smog of words and numbers that various "authorities" provide (at a substantial price). If only our newspapers and schools of journalism saw a reporter's job as something more than that of an accountant of sorts, who tabulates events as if they were sums to be accepted at face value and listed and added up. And if only all of us who go to college and then one or another professional school were encouraged to feel at home with the heart's reasons, the world's ceaseless ambiguities and, not the least, the mind's capacity (given a choice) to say what is obvious and important and right. For the fact is that we are systematically taught to trick ourselves, as well as others; we lose our candor and openness and forthrightness of speech in response to the demands that powerful, if virtually incomprehensible educators make upon us—in their lectures, through the books and articles they assign and the kinds of examinations they insist we take. So it was natural that I would find myself confused and at a loss years after I first met certain migrant farm workers or sharecroppers or Appalachian yeomen. All I had were my theories, my costly and intimidating "training," my wordiness developed in school after school. What I lacked was what I most needed, a photographer's eye, a novelist's ear, a poet's responsiveness to sights and sounds.

We cannot, most of us, take good pictures or write good stories or summon words in ways that illuminate and entrance; but as men or women who once were children, we most certainly can look and listen and admit to amusement or anger or surprise. And we can speak our minds, let others know how we feel, what we feel—unless, that is, we happen to take stock of the "situation" around us and decide that it is dangerous to do just that, in which case we stop seeing things and shut up, or learn to speak the double talk that threatens no one and leaves us "secure," if virtually scared of our own shadows. Thus do children "grow up" and learn to surrender and stop living—and become safely (so far as our society is concerned) "mature" and "adult." So, I will say that in this book Dwayne Walls shows himself to be still a certain kind of child, an alive, questioning child; and I hope he will not mind that way of putting things.

Not far from the county in North Carolina that he knows so well and describes so vividly in the pages ahead, I came to know a poor black family whose son left the South for reasons quite other than those that prompt travelers on the Chickenbone Special. The young man was "found" by a "scout" and enabled to attend Harvard College, where I met him. I went back with him one spring (a special kind of journey, no doubt about that), and later, when both of us were safely back in Cambridge, Massachusetts, he could allow himself at least a brief tirade, and not the politically indignant one that, I fear, I assumed and expected: "I hate what poverty has done to my people, to my own parents. I hate what the white man has done to the black man in the South—and the North. But every time I go home, I get all mixed up. I see the misery, but I see my father's intelligence and his cleverness and his 'psychological acuity,' as those professors of mine call it.

Introduction

I see my mother's humor, her kindness, her toughness. And then I don't know what to think. On the way North I try to understand them; that's what we're taught to do in college—understand, understand. But what do college professors know about the spirit my mother has, or my father? Professors know facts, and they come up with a lot of theories. Even anthropologists are like that: they describe towns and houses and 'customs,' and then they come up with a dozen or so 'conclusions'; but they don't tell the people who read their books what goes on inside people—in their souls, I mean, not their 'minds.'

"I've been reading Flannery O'Connor in my English course. She was a white lady from down in Georgia, a maiden lady, I gather, who died very young. What does she know about the black man, I wondered. Well, she knows about everyone who's living in the rural South, I know that since I've read her. In fact, she knows about everyone who's alive and trying to stay alive; I could say that, too. When I read a story of hers about some weird Georgia cracker, I begin to forget they are what I just said, weird Georgia crackers. They're my aunt, who laughs with tears in her eyes; and my grandfather, who got drunk every weekend and talked about 'fighting patience'—as what the nigger needs; and my cousin who's old enough to be my uncle, and all his tricks and clever sayings—'smart-aleck remarks,' the bossman used to call them, but he missed them when he didn't hear them for a while, because he used to tease my cousin. He used to say: 'When are we going to get another smart-aleck remark out of you?' Sometimes I remember all that, my family and how they lived down South and what they said and did—and then I'll decide I knew more about my 'people,' my 'race,' when I was a child than I'll ever learn from reading all these 'black studies' books I push my way through."

The young Southern emigree has never really been tempted by the social sciences, has instead developed an interest in something called "history and literature"; and so perhaps he can be considered "prejudiced" in favor of writers like Miss O'Connor and Ralph Ellison, or historians like C. Vann Woodward or T. Harry Williams. Maybe, too, he is giving up some of his angry political concerns for those more "literary" (if not obscure) preoccupations that some social critics and political ideologues find to be treacherous signs of a "sellout," a "brainwashing," a surrender to a "power structure." Yet that man has developed no loss of social indignation, no progressive indifference to the political and economic injustices he knew for years and years—and still knows, as a son does rather than a proud book reader and occasional member of this or that "cause." I think he simply senses in the South's moral complexities and racial tragedies something utterly worthy of the mind's capacity for dedicated portrayal—which is to say, he believes it is no accident that the South has produced such intense, formidable, ambitious novelists and storytellers and playwrights and journalists and historians.

Out of that tradition, and worthy of it, comes Dwayne Walls, another such writer, observer, essayist. He tells us about poor rural blacks who reluctantly head for ghettos that are no Promised Land at all; but even more, he brings alive particular human beings

Introduction

who share with all other human beings the knowledge of fear, the experience of dread, the surge that hope can bring, and the confusion that the mind's various maneuvers can also bring. One must continually get angrily "defensive" (as, I suppose, some psychiatrists would interpret the "reaction") about writers like Mr. Walls—because they are not the people that other people, eager, swinging, clever, wordy, self-consciously "aware" and proudly "educated," rush to for explanations, ideas, programs, solutions and, that word of words these days, "insights." Nor is it likely that this book will shock inert consciences, surprise bored and worldly experts, inflame even further already outraged activists. There is a quietness to the effort Mr. Walls makes, a slowness to his manner of approach. He wants drama to emerge from the ways of others, rather than to be of his own doing. He wants us to grow by feeling others grow on us. And I presume that, good writer and sensitive man that he is, he wants us to become once again not knowing and smart and informed, but uncertain, embarrassed, amused, and at a certain loss about various things—"states of mind" that one can only be grateful for and, these days, almost relieved to find still possible.

THE CHICKENBONE SPECIAL

Chapter One
TAKING A RIDE

Otis Gibson sat on the cool side of the porch, looking across the little cotton patch to the cornfield beyond. Watching the corn, he could tell when the next breeze was coming by following the ripples as the wind rolled across the corn rows toward the house.

Otis was not a tall man, and the way he slumped in the wheelchair made him look much like a young boy lolling away a lazy afternoon. His bare feet were stretched out nearly to the edge of the little porch. His trousers were pulled up over his loins and left unfastened for his and his family's convenience. His shirt was only partially buttoned across the chest. His body, which he could not control entirely, was canted to one side, so that he had to twist his neck to keep his head in an upright position. Still, half of his nut-brown face seemed to sag to the right as his body did, and tiny rivulets of sweat rolled naturally toward his right chin, where they were joined by a barely perceptible overflow of saliva at the lower corner of his mouth. Small particles of food stuck to his lips because he had insisted on using the napkin himself after his noon meal, instead of allowing his wife to brush off his chin.

It was late afternoon, and Otis still had not made up his mind whether to shave. He had been thinking about it for a long time now, maybe an hour or more. The trouble was, he was not exactly straight on what day it was, and it was important to know what day it was before he could decide about the shave. Sometimes he thought that was the most bothersome thing about the stroke—not the wheelchair and the dead right arm and the dead right leg, but the trouble in his head.

Most of the time he could think straight. He knew what he wanted. But sometimes he could not say it. Like the other day, when he wanted a drink of water. Donnie had had to make three or four trips into the house bringing things out before he finally understood what Otis wanted. Otis had thought he said water every time. Finally, all he could do was nod when Donnie guessed right.

But there were times, like today, when Otis himself could not understand what his mind was saying. He wanted to be shaved for Sunday. He could not go to church—not in the wheelchair. But some of the folks might come by, and he wanted to be shaved and dressed.

Was it yesterday that Donnie had graduated? Or the day before? It must have been last night, and that meant today was either Friday or Saturday. He could not be sure, but he reckoned that was close enough.

"If it's Saturday," he reasoned, "I better shave because there won't be no time in the morning. If it's Friday, then I might as well shave anyway because everybody will be busy tomorrow."

Besides, he decided, the shave would last.

Having made his decision to shave, Otis twisted

slightly in the wheelchair so his voice would carry through the screen door into the back of the house.

"Donnie," he called, "come shave me."

Calling his youngest son to shave him was as natural to Otis Gibson as picking up a razor would be to any other man. For more than a year now, since that morning when they had found him slumped over the side of the bed, Otis had relied on Donnie for almost everything, it seemed, except breathing.

The Gibsons—Otis and Julia and their seven children—always had been a close family. Close in a way that a lot of people could never understand. The children, for example, had grown up never using the words *mama* and *daddy*. To them, Otis had been "Otis," and Julia had been "Julia." But there seemed to be a special bond between Otis and his youngest. Everybody in the family had recognized it years ago, long before Otis's stroke in March of 1968. The bond had strengthened after Otis came home from the hospital. Now, it seemed to Otis, Donnie had become his right arm and his right leg, and sometimes, he knew, even part of his head. Donnie shaved him and took him to the new bathroom they had put in the house after he came home. When he was not in school, Donnie fed and even cooked for Otis sometimes. Julia had her hands full looking after the farm and the grandbabies, and so Donnie had learned to cook—mostly rice and fried chicken—and to help with the washing.

Donnie was the one who stayed home on Sunday so the rest of the family could go to church. At first Donnie and Julia had taken turns on that. But then Donnie sent off for a Bible-study course; after that he stayed home Sundays, working his Sunday-school lesson with Otis. He would read the lesson, and then fill out the questions and mail it off.

Donnie was the one who knew best how to figure out what Otis wanted when Otis could not talk plain; and he was the one with the patience to keep on guessing and trying and running back and forth when he could not figure it out.

It was Donnie who nailed the board across Otis's favorite side of the front porch so the wheelchair would not roll off. And it was Donnie who had put up the railing next to Otis's good left hand, a place for Otis to lay his pipe and tobacco within easy reach.

Otis was reaching for the pipe when it occurred to him that Donnie was taking a long time getting the razor and soap together.

"Donnie," he called again.

"Be right there, Otis."

Otis did not notice a few minutes later that Donnie came to the porch empty-handed.

"I'm gonna give you the shave later," Donnie said. "But I want to talk to you first, Otis."

"What you want to talk about?" Otis asked.

Donnie pulled up the chair facing Otis and turned his head away, looking toward the cornfield. Sitting there together, the two of them could not have been mistaken for anything but father and son. Donnie, at 5 feet 10 inches, was slightly taller than Otis, and he was not quite as muscular. His color was like his mother's, lighter than Otis's color. But there was a striking resemblance to his father in other respects. He had the same broad shoulders and the same face—an open, guileless face that seemed always to be on the brink of a smile. He had his father's receding hairline; and the lips, which seemed perfectly shaped, were the same as his father's, except that they did not sag to the right.

"This is the last shave I'll be giving you," Donnie said. "After today, somebody else will have to shave you. Jessie, maybe." Jessie, a year older than Donnie, was the only other child living at home, not counting the grandbabies.

"What you talking about?" Otis asked.

"I'm through school now, Otis, and I'm taking a ride tomorrow."

If Otis had been still a normal man, if his head had been as clear as it once was, the phrase would have registered in an instant. Almost anybody in Williamsburg County, South Carolina, knows what it means—almost anybody who is black, and who has raised a son or a daughter to the age of sixteen or seventeen.

Otis Gibson was a black man; he had heard the phrase, or something like it, at least five times in recent years. But now it left him confused.

"Ride? Ride where?" he asked.

"*New* York," Donnie said, stressing the first word in that lilting, calypso-like speech common to all black people and many whites in the South Carolina low country. "I'm going to *New* York."

Otis Gibson had seen his three daughters and two of his four sons leave home as soon as they got out of high school. He had seen countless brothers and sisters and nieces and nephews leave, until it seemed that there would be none of his kin left to ease his passage into old age. Once, a long time ago, he had dreamed of the far-off day when he could turn the farm over to his sons, give up the scuffle of public work, and live out his days in peace. Now, in his prime, he was a cripple who couldn't look after himself and couldn't even think straight. He couldn't work any more. The farm was about shot. Most of his kin were gone.

"And, oh, Lord Jesus," he thought, "now we're losing Donnie, too."

Waiting on the porch for Donnie to bring the razor and shaving soap, Otis had never before felt so alone, so helpless. He held back the tears until Donnie had finished shaving him.

Chapter Two

LET NEW YORK BE LIKE I THINK IT IS

Raymond Carl Gibson, who has been called "Donnie" for as long as he can remember and for no apparent reason, had known for five days that he would be leaving Williamsburg County as soon as he got his diploma. He had known it and dreaded it—dreaded it and yet found it impossible to hold back a feeling of excitement within himself.

Williamsburg County, the city of Kingstree, the little farm near the community of Salters, the church up the road and the school in Greeleyville a few miles away—

all this was home to Donnie. Without ever really thinking much about it, he knew that it had been a good home for his seventeen years. He had never wanted to live anywhere else.

There had been times when he wanted to travel. Once, just after he had started high school, he saw a picture post card that his brother Leon had sent from Hawaii, where he was stationed. He said to himself then that someday he wanted to go to Hawaii. Twice, he had been to Columbia, the state capital, with the high-school chorus. He thought it would be great to spend a week there sometime. But those things could wait. He figured he would get drafted in a year or two, and that would give him a chance to do all the traveling he wanted.

Donnie had never bothered looking beyond the draft; nor had he done any real planning at all. He had not made a deliberate, conscious decision to stay in the county when he began applying for a job in April. He did it because that was the normal thing to do, because it did not occur to him not to do it. He knew that jobs were scarce in Williamsburg and surrounding counties, even if he did not know the awful statistic. But he could not think of himself as not getting a job. He had better-than-average grades in school, and in six weeks he would have a diploma. That ought to count for something.

He went first to Albany Felt, the textile mill in Saint Stephen, where Jessie worked. Then he went to the Douglas plant at Saint Stephen and to Georgia Pacific's office at Russellville. The routine had been the same at each place. He filled out the application, turned it in, and was told that there were no foreseeable openings but that he would be contacted if any suitable openings came up.

He had heard nothing from the applications when Renea called from New York the Sunday before graduation.

What was he going to do after graduation, Renea wanted to know.

Donnie told her about the applications, and the story was a familiar one to his sister. It could have been her 1965 graduation all over again. She forced back the anger.

"Donnie," she said, "if you ain't heard anything by now, you ain't gonna hear. Why don't you come to New York?"

There were jobs available, she told him, and he could live with her until he got work. If he was coming, though, he ought to come as soon as he could. The New York high schools would not graduate until two weeks after those in Williamsburg County. He ought to start applying before then.

"I don't know," Donnie said. "The man at Saint Stephen said something might come up."

"Well, why don't you just come up and visit for a while. I'll send you the money. That's your graduation present."

They left it that way. If he decided to come, he would call back and she would send the money.

Donnie thought about it a long time that night. At the baccalaureate service that day, he had talked with some of the boys who were going North. He knew at least ten in his class who were leaving the day they got their diplomas.

He thought about New York. He wanted to see Central Park almost as much as he wanted to see Hawaii. There would be a chance to see the Mets and all the skyscrapers.

He thought about Archie and Leon. Both of them had had to drive all the way to Thomasville up in North Carolina, where Otis worked, to find jobs after they got out of school and before they moved to New York. Belle had found a job in Fayetteville, and then moved to New York. She was the one who was always taking pictures and sending them back home. Everywhere she went, she was always taking pictures.

He thought about Jessie. Jessie had graduated in 1968 and had filled out applications at six different places. It was not until October that he finally got a job, and that was almost by accident. Albany Felt had not called Jessie. Jessie had just gone down there one Saturday morning and talked with the superintendent. He had been waiting a long time, Jessie told the man, and he needed a job. He had a sick daddy at home.

Jessie went to work the next Tuesday in the spinning room at $1.70 an hour. He was making $1.85 now, but he was bringing home only $63 a week, unless he got overtime. He worked the second shift, and he had to drive nearly sixty miles a day—twenty-eight miles each way. In New York, Donnie knew, jobs were paying $2 and $3 an hour.

Donnie thought about the farm and Otis and Julia. It was not much of a farm any more—a good home, a good place to live, but not much of a farm. He sure could not make a living working the farm.

The Gibson farm is a modest, asbestos-sided house with eight small rooms, a large shade tree, a small chinaberry tree, a vegetable garden, and 8.2 acres of sandy loam on the back side of a larger farm whose owner has been better able to survive the failing economy of small farms. To get there you turn off the paved country road and follow a sandy lane for about a quarter of a mile, past hogpens and tobacco barns, and through the cornfield.

The Gibsons inherited the farm when Julia's father died in 1937, and technically part of it belonged to Julia's eleven brothers and sisters. But they were all gone by then, living in Richmond and Philadelphia and New York. Julia and Otis had raised her two youngest brothers, and with their share the Gibsons owned outright a little over three acres. But the others had signed over the rest of the property for the Gibsons to live on, and Otis had built the house there in 1955.

Although the farm had not supported the family for several years, it was a source of extra income. Julia and the kids did the farming. Otis had given up full-time farming in 1952 to take public work. He tried sawmilling for one year and then got a job with the railroad. When the railroad cut back its staff in 1958, Otis finally found a job with a furniture plant up in North Carolina. He boarded up there through the week and came home on weekends to help Julia with the farm. It was a long way to drive, but it paid pretty good money—$45 and $50 a week even without overtime. He was working there when he had the stroke.

Julia is a big woman, square-shouldered and thickly built—a woman who can do a man's job because she has never known anything else but work. She managed pretty well on the farm at first. They had a full acre of tobacco allotment and a three-acre cotton allotment. She had the mule and the kids at home to help, and in a good year she could clear maybe $600 to $800. But the government kept cutting back the tobacco allotment, and one year she planted only two acres of cotton and lost the other acre in the allotment. It had got harder and harder to make the crop as the children grew up and left home. She found that her pace was falling away, especially after a day in the fields. The veins on her legs bulged to the point where they looked as if they would burst in places. When Otis took sick last year she gave up farming and rented out to a neighbor what was left of the tobacco and cotton allotments.

The tobacco, down now to just over half an acre, was rented for fifteen cents per pound. If the man made a good crop, Julia would get $141 in rent. The two acres of cotton would bring in $15 an acre in rent. She would be paid in the fall, when the crops were harvested.

No, Donnie knew he did not want to farm. But he knew also that he could not wait around for months, as Jessie had done, hoping for a job to open up. Except for the little bit of rent money, the money Julia got from New York for keeping the grandbabies, and what Jessie paid in board, all the money coming in now was Otis's Social Security check. That was $119 a month. But it would be cut as soon as Donnie left home or went to work.

New York. Brooklyn. Archie and Leon seemed to be doing all right. The girls, too. Geraldine didn't like living up there. He knew that. She had come home last year to look for a job and finally had gone back. He figured the others didn't like it either. All of them wanted to come back someday.

But I don't have to like it, Donnie reasoned. I don't have to stay. I can visit, and if I find a job I'll take it. If I don't like it, I'll come home. I ought to come home anyway if Jessie passes the draft. At least I can be earning some money instead of waiting for a job.

Donnie had made up his mind by the time he drifted off to sleep that Sunday night, and he told Julia the next afternoon.

Julia was on the porch by herself when Donnie got home from school. He would tell her now, because he did not want to tell Otis yet.

"Julia, I'm going up the road," he said.

"You've made up your mind, have you?"

"Yes'm," Donnie said, "I reckon I have."

"But you done put in for a job down here," Julia said. "What you gonna do about that?"

"That's been nearly two months ago," Donnie said. "Nobody has called yet, and it don't look like anybody is gonna call. But if somebody calls, I'll come back, and if Jessie passes the draft, I'll come back."

When she tried later to remember what she had said and how she had felt that afternoon, Julia found that the two things were different.

What she had said to herself was, "Lord, I don't want

him to go. I really don't want him to go. What am I gonna do without him? When I get ready to go to tend to business, I won't have no one to stay with Otis. When I get ready to go to the store, I won't have no one to stay with him. And when I get ready to go to church, I won't have no one to stay with him."

But she knew her son, and she knew there was no need to try to talk him out of it. And so she also said to herself, "I'll do the best I can. I'll make the best of it I can."

To Donnie she said, "Donnie, I wish you wouldn't go. Not right now."

"Jessie'll be here," Donnie said. "And if he passes the draft, I'll come back."

So it was settled. They called Renea that night. The only thing now was to tell Otis. Donnie worried all week about that, and kept putting it off.

The $35 money order from Renea came Thursday, the day of graduation, and Donnie decided he would leave on Friday. The commencement program Thursday night was just the ceremony; the seniors had to go back Friday morning to pick up their diplomas. He would take the afternoon train on Friday.

Donnie had thought about taking the bus. But Julia insisted on the train, although it was more expensive.

"That bus makes too many stops," she told him. "I don't want you wandering around no bus stations getting lost or getting left behind or maybe getting into trouble. You get on that train in Kingstree and you don't have to get off till you make New York. And Renea'll be waiting for you there."

It was Julia's idea also to change wallets. She

remembered the story Archie had told once about this man in New York who had had his wallet stolen by a pickpocket who just slit the man's pocket with a razor and pulled the wallet right out.

Donnie's old wallet was a good one. But a couple of years ago, he had made some money priming tobacco and bought this special wallet—a burglarproof wallet, it was called, and it cost $5.50. It was good leather, the kind that folds longways so it sticks partly out of your pocket, unless you carry it in your coat pocket. But the thing was, it had a thick chain through a hole in one corner and the chain had a ring on the end that you ran your belt through. If anybody tried to get that wallet they'd have to cut the chain.

So Donnie took all the pictures and cards and things out of the old wallet and put it into one of the suitcases he would take. "If this thing is burglarproof," he said of the new wallet, "I'll give it a real test in New York."

Thursday night, Donnie came home from commencement still worried about how to tell Otis and nervous about leaving the next day. He knew he needed some help.

Normally, Donnie's prayers were much like those of any other teen-ager of moderate religious bent—simple and quick, the carry-over phrases learned as a child and spoken absently and in his mind, not aloud. Sometimes, a great many times lately, he forgot to perform even that much.

When he needed real help, though, it was different. And now he needed help.

When he had finished changing into pajamas, he knelt at the foot of the bed—something he had not done for a long time—and let his forehead drop to his hands clasped at the edge of the mattress.

"Dear God," he said, and this time the words passed through moving lips, "Dear God, please help me. Help me to tell Otis and help me in New York. Please let everything work out all right. Let New York be like I think it is. Don't let me be disappointed. Please don't let me get in no trouble. . . ."

There was more, but then, almost as if he couldn't help it, he went back to the same pleas and the words tumbled out over and over in the same sentences.

"Please, please, Dear God, please . . ."

Donnie was not sure, but he thought he felt better when he finally climbed under the sheet. He thought about that prayer the next day.

Julia had started washing his clothes and packing his bags Friday morning, but the washing machine broke down. She took his clothes into town later to do them at the laundry. By then it was too late to catch the Friday train. They decided he would take the Saturday train, and Donnie was sitting at the kitchen table trying to figure out how he was going to tell Otis when Otis called to come and shave him.

Neither of them said much during the shave. Otis had said one thing: "You know you've always got a home to come back to, Donnie."

When the shave was finished Donnie knew he had not said what he wanted to say. He had not said any of it. He had not even said good-by to Otis, and he knew already that he could not face Otis again in the morning.

"Either I'll cry or he'll cry," Donnie thought. "I don't want to cry, and I don't want to see him cry."

So when Donnie and Julia and Jessie left for the train station Saturday morning, Donnie went out the back door to where Jessie was washing the car.

Otis saw them leave in the car, and he was glad Donnie had not stopped at the wheelchair. Otis was sitting on the cool side of the front porch, looking toward the cornfield and not really seeing it.

Chapter Three

HEAVEN, HELL AND BALTIMORE

The Friday that Donnie Gibson gave his father the last shave was a painful day also for the congregation of Saint Stephen Baptist Church in the little community of Mayflower, 350 miles or so northeast of the Gibson home.

The church is not large enough to afford a full-time pastor any more. The Reverend Sidney W. Williams, who rides circuit on several rural churches in the area, preaches at Saint Stephen one Sunday of every month. The other Sundays, and on each Friday night before the preaching Sunday, the church officers conduct Sunday school and prayer meetings.

Because the Friday-night meeting also is the time

when the congregation discusses church business affairs, it is usually presided over by Brother Ernest A. Turner, the church secretary.

"As you all know," Brother Turner said, opening the business portion of the meeting, "we are losing our assistant secretary. Sister Georgia Mae Perry graduates this year, and like so many others in our community, she has got to go North to make a living. She's going to be leaving right after graduation, so we've got to handle the matter tonight because this will be the last business session that she will attend."

Brother Turner paused to look over the little gathering and quickly spotted Georgia Mae in the third row.

"At this time," Brother Turner said, "I would like to ask Sister Perry if she will kindly excuse us while the congregation considers this matter."

Nervous and a little bit embarrassed, Georgia Mae left her seat and tiptoed along the aisle and out the door at the front of the church.

"Now, brothers and sisters, what I want to talk to you about, what I want to put before you, is a matter of money," Brother Turner began.

"As you know, Georgia Mae has been our assistant secretary for two years. And she's done a good job in a trying time. She has finished screening the church roll, the first time that we've done that. She's helped look after things, and she's been a big help to me.

"Now, Georgia Mae is going to be leaving pretty soon, and she don't have a job up North and she is going to need all the money she can get. What I want to propose is that instead of paying her just for the six months of this year that she has held the job, well, we ought to go ahead and pay her for a full year as a going-away present, and in gratitude for her service to this church. Anybody want to make a motion on that?"

There was perhaps half a minute of silence while the congregation thought it over. "I motion it," one of the sisters said.

The vote was unanimous among the congregation, and Brother Turner directed a youngster sitting near the back to escort Sister Perry back into the church.

"Sister Perry," Brother Turner told her, "would you please write down in the minutes of this meeting that the congregation of Saint Stephen Baptist Church has voted unanimous to accept the resignation of the church's assistant secretary as of—you can write in the date later when you get it worked out—and to pay said assistant secretary a full year's pay instead of the six months' pay she would be otherwise entitled to. And please write down further that the said congregation expresses its gratitude and its best wishes and our continued prayers to the assistant secretary as she leaves this fine community."

Georgia Mae's salary was $25 a year. The extra $12.50 was not much, but it was more than she had counted on. She meant it when she gave the congregation her brief thanks.

Ernest Turner also felt pretty good that night. He was glad the church had gone along with the extra salary for Georgia Mae. It was the church's place to help Georgia Mae because she was a church employee. But if this thing of moving North didn't stop pretty soon, Ernest knew, there would not be any community or even a church much longer.

Except in the minds of its citizens, the community of Mayflower already had ceased to exist in name that summer of 1969. It was being held together mostly by the church and the determined efforts of a few men like Ernest Turner.

Mayflower, an isolated farm community thirteen miles south of Warrenton, North Carolina, sits in the southern end of Warren County, near the Franklin County line, where Highway 58 leaves Inez, heading south toward Rocky Mount. About eight miles south of Inez, the highway crosses the county line at Shocco Creek, and that is the southern boundary of Mayflower. The center of the community is near the point where a paved secondary road leads off eastward to a dead end about four miles away. The church, Ernest Turner's store and service station, and the old school building sitting up on the hill between the church and the store are Mayflower's main landmarks.

The community got its name from the little three-room school that provided all the education most of its citizens ever got during the thirty to forty years of the school's existence. When the school was closed by the county board in the mid-sixties, the church became the center of the community, and some of the folks who lived there started calling it the "Saint Stephen community."

The new name has caught on pretty well, although the white people in Warrenton, the county seat, still call it Inez, because they figure it is just a part of the white community by that name up the road.

Almost anybody who remembers when a plow was pulled by mule instead of by tractor can remember when Mayflower was a busy community of maybe a hundred families, most of whom owned their land and farmed it the best they could. It was not a wealthy community. It was, in fact, a very poor one. But it was not poor in spirit. The people worked hard and shared their pain and their joy, and what little fleeting wealth they might own.

If all its people could have made a decent living there, Mayflower would have been just about the best place this side of Heaven for most of them. It was a place where life was slow and ordered, where a man had to work hard but knew a time of peace when the work was done. It was a place where you knew and loved and trusted your neighbors, and knew also that you could count on them in time of need. It was the kind of place a man cannot understand and appreciate unless he is a farmer who has sat on his porch late of an evening, after a good day in the fields, and dozed to the music of whippoorwills and bobwhites.

But most of the people in Mayflower could not make a decent living there, and so they left. They left reluctantly, painfully, hoping to the last minute they would not have to leave. But they left Mayflower and Marmaduke, Embro and Arcola, and a place called Lickskillet. They left Warren County the way they left every other county in tobacco country—first by the tens, then by the hundreds, and finally by the thousands. One day a welfare case worker heard it, and then another and another; and it was passed on to the welfare director, who passed it on to a newspaper, who passed it on to the nation: "These people know only three places to go: Heaven, Hell and Baltimore."

They went to Baltimore and Washington and New York City, and a hundred places between Washington and New York, places they had never been to but had begun to hear about more and more. Baltimore—or Washington or New York or Newark—was surely the land of milk and honey, the Promised Land. The people knew it because somebody who had gone North before had come back to tell them. So maybe the fancy car he was driving was a rental car, or one he had borrowed or was breaking his back to pay for. So maybe it was not all that great up there. So what? He had a job, didn't he? And that's better than you can say for down here, ain't it?

For some it *was* the Promised Land, and the promise was kept. They got decent jobs, and their kids got a decent eduction. These poor, ignorant blacks—these products of a second-rate school system—went North to become schoolteachers and police captains and civil servants. They became doctors and lawyers, and even nuclear physicists. More important to the folks back home, they got jobs—forty-hour jobs, guaranteed against crop failure, with time and a half for overtime.

But gradually it became clear that Baltimore and Hell often were the same place. The word began trickling back to the farms: stay where you are. The city is no place for people like us. The city is changing. You ain't gonna like it.

Man, it ain't human up there.

The word was carried back first by the older people, those who had been in the spearhead of the exodus, those who had survived and made a place for themselves, only to give in finally to that eternal longing to chuck it all and get back home again—to a place where a man could live in peace and raise his kids the way they ought to be raised. A strange thing for a black man to say of the South.

The word came back also in the battered spirit of the youngsters, the remnants of the later exodus. They had left, piss-and-vinegar proud, filled with post-card visions of what the city was supposed to be. They were confident, and they were educated—a fact that had been assured and certified by the stolid white farmers who run the South's rural schools. They could make it. But somehow they did not make it, or could not take it. They learned that the cities had become bloated with people like themselves, that the cities could not digest any more of them. They were untrained and uneducated, they discovered, and highly visible. Therefore they did not live in luxury apartments, drive fancy cars, prowl the classy nightspots. They got jobs, most of them, but only the worst jobs. They lived in slums and rode buses and subways. They left home before daylight and got home again after dark. And they began locking their doors, a thing they had never done at home. When they could afford to drink, they drank in grimy bars or at the kitchen table.

And when they could not take it any more, they bought bus tickets with their last paycheck and spent the long ride South staring at the face reflected in the bus window. The land—the strange, grimy Northern land—sped backward past the window, sucking away the tension and the frustration of the passengers. Only when the bus neared home did the passengers begin to think of their pride, to dream up stories to salvage it. They had been laid off. They had got sick. They knew the folks at home needed them. They were between jobs, and were planning to go back as soon as things picked up a little. They had come back only to help the family make this year's tobacco crop. Just taking a little vacation, man. Pretty soon, I'll be going back.

But the people at home knew; they had got the word. And still their answer was the same: at least there are jobs in the city. So the people kept right on leaving, more fearful perhaps, but driven nonetheless by the same desperate need: a job.

They left by bus, by train, by old family car crawling along the highways, crablike, its front end clinging to the center line and the rear end grabbing for the shoulder of the pavement. But many of them did not own cars, and so the professional hustler came along. He did own a car, or a truck, and for a fee he would haul a family to any ghetto in the nation. For another fee he sometimes could put a man onto a job in the city.

The people went North and prospered, and sent back home for relatives—sometimes even for long-dead relatives, who were disinterred and shipped North for reburial because North was home now, and a man likes to have his kin buried at home.

They went North and died, peacefully or violently, and came home in interstate shipping caskets in such numbers that little country churches began to feel a population explosion in their graveyards. The deacons and elders took stock of the diminishing burial ground and imposed plot fees on departed brethren who had not been active members of the congregation. Some of the South's black undertakers sent word to some of the North's black undertakers to encourage their clients to bury the dead where they died, And still the bodies came back.

The people went North and did not prosper, but stayed to exist on public welfare, reasoning that if a family has to take welfare, it is better to take it in the North at $50 or $60 a head than in the South at $30 a head or less.

Young black girls went North in relative innocence, conceived babies in reckless flight from loneliness, bore them in despair and resignation, took them back South for mama to raise and then returned to the cities, often to bear more babies. Marriage frequently did not change the pattern. Mama still got the babies to raise because young married migrants could not afford an apartment large enough for children unless the mother worked. And even so, there was no one to care for the babies. Besides, the city was no place to raise children.

The people left, and in their leaving made it necessary for others to leave. Deprived of cheap labor, the farmers began turning to machinery, which began replacing the remaining cheap labor.

The people who left, and who continue to leave, are commonly regarded as the best ones—the strongest, the healthiest, the most industrious, the cream of the crop. The people left behind are the crippled, the very young and the very old—and, by debatable inference, the weakest. They have been described at times as "the damned scrubs" (by rural white farmers), and as the end result of the weak breeding the weak (by learned doctors of philosophy).

The places left behind are the fields abandoned to the weeds and honeysuckle, and the legal recourse of a mortgage holder. Moldering houses become palatial homes for bats and mice, and then trysting places for hungry cats and human lust. Commerce begins to dry up, first in the country stores—romanticized as genuine pieces of Americana—where credit and usury and insensate avarice were blessed by Christian ethic; then in the smug little towns whose leading citizens clung—still cling—to the nineteenth century and proclaimed—still proclaim—that everything will be all right if only local government can be left alone to solve local problems.

Worst of all, perhaps, the local institutions—the molds that shape individuals into communities—wither and crumble. Clubs and churches are decimated year after year, until finally there is no club and no church remaining.

In Mayflower a decade ago, the Community Development Club was strong enough, even after ten years of heavy out-migration, to win a statewide contest three years in a row for its constructive influence in the community. It got college loans for its high-school graduates, home-repair and home-construction loans. It mustered every family in some sort of activity—encouraging truck crops and finding markets for them, cleaning up the yards and roadsides, providing recreation for the youngsters.

Today, the club is only a scrapbook of fading pictures, ribbons, newspaper clippings and memories.

Mayflower still has its church, and it is the pride and the joy, the giver of life to the citizens of Mayflower. But even the church is threatened with extinction. Already, some nearby churches have begun to combine their holiday services—occasionally with Baptists and Methodists worshiping together. There is a vague awareness among the people that someday, small churches of like denomination—churches such as Shady Grove and Saint Stephen and Greater Lovely Hill—will have to merge if they expect to survive.

The congregation at Saint Stephen is determined that it will survive if such a merger must come. To that end, they have poured into the church in recent years all the love and work and money that they could muster. Four classrooms have been added onto the back of the building. A kitchen and an indoor bath were built in the basement. A new roof was put down. The floors were repaired, and a red carpet was laid down along both aisles. A deep well and a pump were added at a cost of more than $1,300.

The church's white clapboard siding always looks freshly painted. But late August of every year, when the letters have gone out to hundreds of addresses across the nation announcing the date of the annual Homecoming Service, is when everything looks its best. The broad lawn stretching back a hundred yards or so from the highway looks its greenest; the shade of the huge oaks in the yard seems most inviting; the cemetery seems at its neatest.

The old bell in the steeple surely peals most clearly when it is calling its far-flung congregation home for a dinner on the grounds. And that is good, because the invitations in recent years have included a message that the church elders would just as soon leave out: "Do to the fact that so many of our members like you had to leave the county or state to fine suitable work it has caused our membership to decline grately in the last few years, for this reason we are asking everyone for a SPECIAL DONATION on that Sunday afternoon. If it is impossible for you to be present please send your donation to Brother E. A. Turner Route 3, Box 121 Warrenton, N.C. Our goal has been set for $1000.00 or more for this Special Homecoming Day."

It pains the congregation to ask for money that way. But the money must be raised. The church must be kept alive, because it is more than a church. It is the bedrock of the community. Because of the space in the church basement, the community has a Head Start program, which provides decent meals for the children and jobs for a few women. The deep well out front does not belong only to the church. It belongs to the community. When Edward Woodward's well ran dry in 1968, he turned to the church. Until he can afford to sink a new well next year or the year after, Edward will load his barrels—one for the house and one for the hogs—into his old pickup truck two or three times a week, and fill them at the church well.

Yes, the church must be kept alive. And it does not ask any more of its Homecoming brothers and sisters than it imposes upon itself. To meet its modest budget, the church requires of its active members monthly dues totaling $4.25 for each man, $2.25 for each woman and $2.00 for each child under eighteen. Each family is asked also to pay $5.00 a year for cemetery upkeep.

That does not bring in a whole lot of money, because the population of Mayflower has dropped in three decades from 100 families to seventy-five to fifty to thirty-five and to twenty-eight, with a head count of about 110 persons, including children. Ten of the families receive welfare, and seven of them live on Social Security.

During the same period, the church enrollment dropped from 700 to 350 to 235 and to 162 persons, including many who have moved away but still maintain an active membership. At the time of its May 1969 business meeting, it had an average church attendance of around sixty-five and a Sunday-school enrollment of forty-nine persons.

Within two weeks, though, the Sunday-school enrollment was to fall by at least twenty-five per cent. Besides Georgia Mae Perry and its four other high-school seniors, the church was losing Creola Alston and her entire family. The church could not afford to lose any of its members. But the brothers and sisters did especially hate to lose Sister Alston.

Chapter Four
THE LAST CROP

Washington Alston was worried and sort of at loose ends when he stopped in at Ernest Turner's store on Christmas Eve of 1968. Wash was close to $2,000 in debt and dead broke. The work was down to near nothing, and farming was about shot. Wash was a big man—over six feet tall. But lately his shoulders had begun to sag, and he moved slower than usual because his legs and his arms felt strangely heavy at the end of a day, and a night's sleep somehow did not seem enough to lighten them. When he talked at all, his heavy bass voice seemed to come from somewhere deeper than normal in his throat. In all his life, Wash's thick lips had never closed over the large front teeth, and he looked as if he were holding a perpetual smile. In years past, this seeming smile was real more often than not because Wash was easygoing and easy to please. Lately, though, the sag of the lower lip gave an impression more of slow wit than ready smile.

For the first time in his life, Wash had gone into public work after he had sold his crop in the fall. He had to do it. By the time he and Ernest had divided the crop, it had brought Wash something like $400 cash money. That would not even feed his family. His wife had spent three months in the hospital, and they had already told her that she would have to come back in the spring to be operated on. So he thought about it for a while and decided to look for public work. If he could find a job and work the farm, too, he might be able to make it.

He did find a job, but it was not much. He worked with a logging crew cutting pulpwood in three or four counties, anywhere they could buy a stand of pines, and hauling it to the yard in Franklin County. At first it was pretty good work. But then the weather turned bad, and he was cut down to two or three days a week, sometimes not even that.

Wash had not worked in a week when Ernest sent word for him to stop by the store.

"Got a feller here wants to talk to you, Wash," Ernest said.

Wash looked at the man and then looked away politely. "Yeah?" and he chuckled. "Hope he ain't bill collecting."

"Nah," Ernest answered. "Says he might have a job for you. Stays up in Washington. Name's Willie Durham."

Wash and Willie Durham exchanged nods, and then Willie looked hard at Wash, the way a preacher stares into the face of a sinner.

Willie hitched up his baggy trousers and adjusted the half-rim glasses on his nose. He stared at the shelf of groceries along the wall for half a minute or so to collect his thoughts, and then turned his fierce stare onto Wash.

"I'm looking for a man," Willie Durham said, and the way he said it he sounded like a preacher.

"Yeah? What kind of man?" Wash asked.

"Working man. Hard-working man. Good man. Steady man. 'pendable man. Don't want no drinking man." With every short burst of words, he slammed the palm of his hand onto the drink box.

"What kind of job you got?" Wash asked him.

"Good job. Steady job. Good money. Regular money. Got a place for you to live, too. Take your whole family."

Wash sipped on the soda the man had paid for and listened to the description of the job and the house, and what it was like up in Washington. And he figured.

The way the man was talking, Wash could not make anywhere near that kind of money farming. He could not farm that much land, even if he had it. "And God knows," he told himself, "I ain't got it."

His own tobacco allotment had been cut two years earlier from 1.9 acres to 1.3. Even with the little patch he farmed on shares with Ernest, it was hardly worth the trouble. He did not have the money and the equipment to get into anything else. Besides, he didn't know anything else but making tobacco.

"I reckon I'm your man," Wash said. Taking a drink now and then did not make him a drinking man, he figured.

"When you want to go to work?" Willie Durham asked.

"Well, I don't reckon I can go today."

"I'll be back for you next week," Willie said. And he was.

They rode up in Willie Durham's car, and Wash went to work New Year's Day of 1969 looking after the linen in a motel in Arlington. After all deductions, he was taking home $85 a week, more money than he had ever thought he would make in his lifetime.

The word spread quickly throughout the little community of Mayflower. Creola and the kids were going to stay until school was out in the summer, and then move to Washington. The Alstons' neighbors took the news pretty badly. They were happy for the Alstons in a way. But Wash and Creola Alston were good people, the kind of folks who made the community what it was and helped hold it together. They were the kind of people the community hated to lose, could not afford to lose.

It is said by the men of Mayflower that Creola Alston is the kind of woman that every man in the community would like his wife to be. But when the men say this, the women of Mayflower do not mind. The unkindest rebuttal they can muster is a reminder that a lot of women in the community would like to have a man as dependable as Wash Alston is.

Creola was a pretty woman when she and Wash were married in 1949. But twenty years of farming and childbearing and hardship had demanded much of her body, almost more than even Creola was capable of giving. Her front teeth were gone now, and the loss of her hair was a constant worry to her. Ten years ago, she had come down with scalp infection brought on by nerves, and the doctor had told her to cut her hair. She cut it and treated her scalp. The infection cleared up, although it came back now and then, but the hair never did grow back. She wore what she had curly and natural, like the Afro cuts that the youngsters were just now beginning to go in for. She was not vain about her hair. But it did bother her, shame her in a way, because somehow she felt that it was not exactly right and proper for an upright woman to wear her hair that short.

When Wash came home Christmas Eve to tell her about the job, she was still weak from the dropsy attack. She had spent three months at Duke University Hospital wondering if she ever would be able to get up and about again. But she had. The doctors had been just wonderful, and they had saved little Hosea, although he would be the last of her eleven children.

But it was not for her physical strength and beauty that the men and the women of Mayflower admired

Creola. It was a whole lot more than that, a lot of things that a man just couldn't put into words. One thing was the way she looked out for that man of hers. Like the sun rose and set on him. And her family. She kept her kids neat and clean, and made them learn manners. They had a lot of manners. And her faith. Other women had faith. But Creola carried hers so well. Lots of women had faith on Sundays, but they wanted everybody to know they had it. Creola had faith all the time, and she didn't care if anybody knew that or not. She didn't show it off. Smart, too. She didn't put a man down the way some women did. She built him up, and the way she would listen and then say something nice, well, it just made a man feel good all over.

Mayflower would lose something when it lost Creola, and Creola knew that she would lose something also. She was feeding the baby when Wash told her about the talk with Willie Durham. "Well, I guess it's God's will," she said, "and if it's God's will, then we'll just go and do the best we can and trust Him to help us and look out for us."

That night she prayed over it and wondered if there was some special reason Willie Durham had come to Ernest's store. On Christmas Eve, of all days.

Washington—the place and her man—was constantly in her prayers during the next five months, the regular prayers every night, and also the special little prayers that she was accustomed to sending up periodically throughout the day. Long ago, Creola had worked out a schedule of daily prayer and Bible reading that she lived by faithfully—once at night before bed and once in the morning. When it was possible, she liked to schedule her morning worship so that it would coincide with the thirty-minute broadcast of the Reverend Oliver Blaine, her favorite radio evangelist. The broadcast came on at 9:30 every morning, and Creola loved to sit by the radio with her Bible and feel for a little while that she was really in the presence of God. Between the two formal worship services, Creola also sent up her impromptu prayers through the day—sometimes asking, sometimes thanking, and often just talking in a sort of mental conversation; for in these prayers she did not have to close her eyes or speak the words aloud, or even stop whatever it was she was doing at the time. Secretly, she believed that these prayers somehow increased her intimacy with God.

In a few weeks, she had pretty well prayed the worry out of her mind and did not think too much about the move to the city, although she still included it in her prayers. She did worry about Wash, though, and she did so miss having him there. She wanted the family to be all together again, to be whole again.

In February, Creola went back to Duke Hospital for the hysterectomy. Ernest and Dottie Turner and the other neighbors looked after the kids, and everything went well. The people were so nice to her that she really did not mind the ten days in the hospital; when she came home, she felt a lot better, although she still had a problem with her blood pressure.

Ernest and Dottie would not hear of her going straight to her house after coming from a warm hospital. They insisted that she stay with them for a few days to rest up some more and get her strength back. Dottie took the children who had been staying with her and

Ernest down to the Alston home the next week to clean it and build a good fire in the stove, and Wash came down from Washington for a couple of days to help her get settled in again.

Spring came and Creola's strength began returning. Her light-brown skin was clear again, and her face was unlined. She thought that, even with the flecks of gray in her hair, she probably looked younger than her forty-one years. She knew that she felt better than she had since she had got pregnant with little Hosea eighteen months ago. Creola felt so good, so blessed to be healthy and up and about again, that she refused to let the worry about moving creep back into her mind.

But then on the last Sunday in May, she was putting on her best white dress to go to church when the forthcoming move forced itself out of the back of her mind and into her thoughts. This was preaching Sunday, she realized, the last preaching Sunday she would be able to spend at her beloved church. The next one would not be until the fourth Sunday in June, and she would be in Washington before then.

Creola never felt closer to God than she felt in church that day. The Reverend Williams's words seemed to come forth just for her ears alone: "I tell you, brothers and sisters, man is fighting his God today. Yes he is. And man can't win. God is all-powerful. He's got the strength of a thousand men. Yes. And God's word says you've got to love God. You can't fight him. You've got to love God. Love God, brothers and sisters, and I tell you—the Book tells you. The Book tells you right here—love God and you gonna win. Love God and He'll lead you along the darkest roads. Yes He will.

He'll help you over the roughest shoals, past unknown perils. Love God, I tell you, brothers and sisters, and you can face the fires of Hell with joy in your heart. Walk the face of this earth without fear of mortal man. . . ."

Creola wished Wash had been there to hear the Reverend Williams's sermon. She knew she had a good husband, a man as good as any woman ever had. But two things pained her an awful lot. Wash would drink on weekends, and he wasn't a churchgoer. He never let his drinking hurt his work. But he did drink too much. She tried to forgive him that. But all she could do about his religion was pray that the Spirit would touch him as it had touched her.

She prayed that someday Wash would start going to church and know the joy she knew that day. Even the hymns seemed to be speaking to her, especially "Ship of Zion." When the Spirit moved Sister Mary, next to her, Creola felt like standing up and shouting with her. Instead, she slipped over slightly in her seat and gently held the sister's arm to keep her from falling when the Spirit left her.

"Great Jehovah," Creola thought, "will I ever find such a wonderful church, such a blessed church as this when I get to Washington?"

Chapter Five

A WOMAN BLESSED

Creola heard the tractor turn off at the main road and followed the steady cough of the Diesel engine as the driver covered the quarter-mile of narrow, twisting road through the woods and past the Alston front yard.

She looked up from her washtub in the back yard as the tractor came around the side of the house and turned into the field. She straightened her back, with her left hand pressing down on her hip. Squinting into the afternoon sun toward the tractor, she recognized Lafayette Turner on the driver's seat.

Lafayette maneuvered the tractor into the near corner of the field, shifted the machine into neutral, and looked back toward the disk harrow to be sure the blades were positioned right. He saw Creola and saluted her with a slow flip of his wrist, two fingers raised to shoulder height, as if he were ordering a couple of sodas at the Tastee-Freeze in town. He pulled back on the hydraulic lever and watched the disks bite into the earth. Satisfied, he turned back to the steering wheel, eased the gearshift into slow drive and began his first pass across the field.

It was a small field, a couple of acres at most. But Lafayette knew it would take him almost until dark to finish it. He was a good driver. But he was careful. He liked to take care of the equipment.

Creola stood watching a while, knowing she ought to get back to the wash and not knowing why her mind would not leave the tractor. It was late—too late in the day to be putting out a wash. But she had so many things to do, so many things to wash in the next few days, that she had to do things as she could. The wash could hang out overnight.

As she stood there, her mind began to drift away from the tractor to the field around it—to the apple tree at the far end of the field, to the berry patch, which used to produce berries but does not any more, to the woods across the road, to the old home place in the bottom beyond the field.

Gradually, she began to identify the strange feeling that had taken hold of her. "Just homesickness, I reckon. We've not even left yet, and already I'm homesick."

Moving had been heavy on her mind since Sunday. Now, watching the tractor, she knew she had to face up to it and accept it. The tractor was opening the land to receive somebody else's seed, to produce somebody else's crop. It was still Alston land. But this year, for the first time since she had moved onto the land twenty years ago—longer than that, since Wash was a baby—the land would not produce an Alston crop.

The land was not good land. It had not been good to the Alstons because it demanded so much and gave back so little. Year after year, they had given it their muscle and their sweat and their fertilizer bought on credit. They gouged it, nursed it and prayed over it, hoping the land could be stirred to renew itself. But the land had grown tired years before the Alstons got it, sapped of its strength in other battles with other planters. Now it could only endure and in its weary endurance wear down the tools and the men who tilled it, until first one and then the other broke or gave up the struggle.

Warren County, North Carolina, where the Alston acres lie, was cotton country before it was tobacco country. It cannot precisely be called a part of the coastal plain because it lies just on the fall line, where the Piedmont plateau drops away from gently rolling red hills to flat sandy loam. Except for patches of sandy soil deposited here and there when the ocean receded eons ago, the land is mostly red clay, more suitable for cotton and grain than for Bright Leaf tobacco. But cotton petered out, and Warren County was becoming tobacco country by default when Washington Alston's father bought his forty-four acres.

The land had beaten down and finally claimed Wash's father when Wash and Creola moved into the home place with Wash's mother in 1949, and still there were too many mouths for the land to feed. Another piece of land had claimed Creola's parents, and the day he took the wedding vows, Wash became in an instant the breadwinner for a family of nine—his mother and himself, Creola and her four younger brothers and sisters, her niece, and her baby by a previous, bad union.

Creola knew and tried always to remember that it is a good man who will accept the responsibility for raising a ready-made family, as Wash had done. Even if she had not loved both of them deeply, Creola would have been eternally grateful to her God and her husband for that blessing. Now, twenty years later to the month, Creola could stand in her humble back yard on the hillside and still feel blessed.

The land had nearly broken them, financially and physically. There were years when it would not yield enough food. Her family had gone hungry at times. She knew that, and it pained her as much now to think about it as it had then to know it.

Yes. They had gone hungry. A child cannot exist for a week on bread and water or bread and weak gravy without being hungry. She knew that, although the children had not complained—except for the little ones, who did not know that a person does not acknowledge hunger, for the same reason he does not believe in the presence of ghosts in the night. To acknowledge hunger is the next thing to accepting it, and the belly pain of it becomes real and unbearable only if hunger is acknowledged and accepted.

The grudging land had not fed them. It had claimed Wash's mother. Time and the land had made the old home place unlivable, and they had gone into debt to build the new place up the hill. The land would not pay the debts. The childbearing and the land's grudging sustenance had nearly broken Creola. It was beginning to wear on Wash.

Still, this little patch of land was theirs. It belonged to them, and it was a part of them. This was home, where the roots were. And they were deep roots. Her entire life had been spent here, on this farm and the nearby tenant farm where she was born, in the little farming community of Mayflower, fifteen miles from the nearest town. This was where she had loved and cried and felt hunger and endured, where she had known the only degree of security she had ever had.

For years, since they were big enough to understand it, Creola had preached to her children over and over that they must study and learn all they could; that they must learn to become independent, to stand on their own two feet; that they must expect to leave the farm someday if they expected to make something of themselves. Now she worried about taking the children off the farm, to a city she had never seen, to a way of life she did not know and frankly feared.

Would the schools be good schools? Would the children have a place to play off the streets? Could she hold them together and shield them from the problems and the temptations of the city until they were old enough to think for themselves? What kind of neighborhood would they live in? What kind of neighbors would they have? Almighty God, would she ever again find the kind of friends and neighbors she had known here?

She watched Lafayette work the disk up close under the apple tree and circle it for another run across the field. "He'll take good care of the land," she thought, dipping into the washtub again. "Me, I'd better get busy looking after my family."

Wash and the boys would be home the first week in June. They would get in on Friday night, and she knew they would want to leave as early as they could get away Saturday morning. She had a lot of work to do before then.

She turned her mind totally to her household chores now, humming and singing to herself one of the songs she had enjoyed so much at church last Sunday: "There is no danger . . . there is no danger . . . in God's world. Get on board . . . get on board this old ship of Zion. . . ."

This year, for the first time in her life, it seemed, Creola knew she would not work a tobacco crop. There would be no trip to the plant beds with the other women in the community.

Chapter Six

THE GOLDEN TOKEN

It is still winter when the planting cycle begins for the tobacco farmer. It is cold and wet and dreary, not the way New York is cold in winter and not the way Florida is wet in summer. It is clammy wet, muddy wet, the way it is when the land and the air are filled with dampness and the skies will neither heat nor freeze the dampness and be done with it.

The dampness clings to the land and everything on the land. In cities like Durham and Richmond and Winston-Salem, it weaves itself into the rich aroma of processed tobacco rising from the cigarette factories. The invisible shroud thus formed drops over the cities, testing the olfactory sense of the natives and reassuring their sense of economic security. In the fields the dampness engulfs the machinery and fertilizes the germ of rust. It bathes and swells the doors of the barns and the privies and the little tenant houses so that the doors will not shut tight, allowing the dampness into the houses. It creeps in on the wind, through the cracks in the doors and windows and walls. It rises on air currents through the floor. It seeps in with the rain that spatters onto the tin roof and trickles into the nail holes and seam cracks, permeating the tenant houses; and then it attacks the tenants.

Along the highways, men who can afford winter vacations begin noticing the strange-looking barns somewhere north of Rocky Mount, where the Interstate ends and U.S. 301 becomes, for a while, the main route for the Florida tourist trade. The barns stand high, as barns are supposed to stand. But they are not big the way barns are supposed to be, because they are not built to hold feed and livestock and equipment, and most of the year they stand empty. Except at harvesttime, when the tobacco must be hung inside them to roast under three or four days of intensive heat, the curing barns stand like tar-paper obelisks, commemorating nothing at all but hard labor.

The tourist sees the barns and then he sees the houses, and he shakes his head and asks of his wife: Which is the barn and which is the house, for Christ's sake? Oh, yeah. That's the house. See the car out front? See the stove and refrigerator and wringer washing machine on the front porch? See the TV antenna?

Now his wife shakes her head and asks of her husband: What kind of people would live in a place like that? Why don't they fix the place up a little? You'd think the least they could do is paint it. Paint doesn't cost that much, for heaven's sake.

Lazy people. Shiftless people. Black people, the husband says. And then he puts them out of his mind. It is more pleasant to think of Florida and the sun, and that great little bar on Collins Avenue.

Inside the farmhouses in the mean winter months, life is a torpid wake for what was and what will be again when spring comes. If he is resourceful and lucky, the farmer can get occasional work and come home to the smell of meat frying on the kitchen stove. He will lie down on a pallet or on the bare floor behind the kitchen stove and let the healing warmth penetrate his arthritic joints, and for a while he can put out of his mind everything else in his world except the heat, the smell and the sound of grease crackling in the pan above him, and the beauty of his wife's hips as she moves about the kitchen. In another room, his children will huddle close to a space heater, staring at a television set turned up deafeningly loud because one of his children is partially deaf from too many colds that turned into too many untreated ear infections. The family will eat and sleep around the stoves. The pallet in the kitchen will become the bed for one of the middle boys. The parents and the babies will sleep in the two beds in the front room. The remaining one or two rooms are not heated, and the older children will sleep there, sometimes three or four to a bed.

The farmer's wife cannot do much laundering in the winter months because the laundry cannot be washed and dried in one day, and then someone must sleep without bedding, and someone will be left without socks or shirt or trousers because there is not enough clothing and bedding to restock the wet laundry. Sometimes the wash will not dry in a week, and the house has about it all winter the smell of urine-soaked bedding and sweat-soaked clothing. The passing tourist does not know that the car and the front-porch appliances are impotent symbols of possession. They do not work except in the sense that each is a refrigerator of sorts in winter and a storage closet in summer. Washing, even personal hygiene, is accomplished by carrying water in from the back-yard well, pouring it into pots on the stove and then pouring it again into wash pans or buckets. The television set does work. But if the family is receiving welfare, they must be careful of the television set. Families who own fifteen-dollar used sets are not considered impoverished enough to draw welfare.

And what of the man who is not resourceful, not lucky? Society, of course, looks after him. He can buy food stamps if he can borrow the money, or he can pick up free surplus commodities once a month if he can find some way to haul them home from the county seat. There is a chance that he can draw welfare. More than likely, he will end up mortgaging himself into bondage for another year by turning to the landlord or the country merchant who carries him or furnishes him if the farmer's landlord approves the credit. For a price only fifteen or twenty per cent higher than it would be if he had cash—plus ten-per-cent interest at settling-up time next fall, of course—the farmer can feed and clothe his family through another winter. The farmer considers his family and his chance of ever bettering his lot. He agrees to plant another crop and takes a bag of groceries home to his wife. The cycle begins again.

The work starts in January with the preparation of

the plant bed. The millions of tiny seeds must be planted safe from the wind and in the warmth of the sun, and so the farmer favors a clearing in the woods or a piece of new ground on the southern edge of the woods. He looks for a gentle slope that will allow good drainage, and scratches out a rectangle in the skin of the black earth—long and narrow and typically equal to about twenty yards of narrow rural highway. He doses the wound liberally with chemicals to kill the weeds and fungus and covers the whole thing carefully with a clear plastic bandage; then he leaves, hoping that he has selected a good spot, that the chemicals will do their work, and that the elements will cooperate with him or, at the very least, do him no harm. He is in debt again now. But this year, maybe this year, he will get good plants, make a good crop, and maybe there will be something left over at settling-up time. There is an old joke in tobacco country in which the smiling landlord announces to his tenant, "Well, Sam. We came out even again. You don't owe me a thing."

In late winter, when the chemicals and the sun's rays have had six weeks or so to cleanse and enrich the soil in the plant bed, the farmer returns to plow the soil again—to feed it, to water it, to spread the seed and change the plastic bandage for one of cheesecloth. Later, when the seeds have taken hold and the little plants have begun to shoot up, he will return to the bed once more to remove the cover altogether.

The time of transplanting begins in Florida in March and moves north with the sun, so that the Georgia-Florida crop has already started ripening when the ancient ritual of transplanting begins in North Carolina and Virginia.

From transplant to harvest is the best time for the tobacco farmer. It is good even though that is when the work is most demanding, when the fields become blistering hot. It is good because there is work to be done, because the farmer has survived another winter to rejoice in the sunlight. It is a time when family and neighbor work together, sharing labor and meager equipment. While the men ready the fields to receive the plants, the women and children remove the young shoots from the plant bed and prepare them for transplanting.

Alternately squatting among the plants and bending in that peculiar stoop that black mothers of the fields pass on to generations of daughters—feet planted wide, knees almost straight, body bent in a right angle at the hip, back horizontal to the ground—the women work rhythmically through the beds. The tender plants must be pulled gently from the soil and examined for maturity and health. The damaged plants must be discarded, along with those whose oversize leaves will block the sun's rays from the plant stem.

The good plants are shaken lightly to remove the old soil and carefully stacked for the planters.

The youngsters work more slowly than the women, partly because of inexperience and partly because of romance. Even in good plant beds the tobacco shoots sometimes are born with a tiny vine clinging to them. These infected shoots also must be discarded, and the search for them is a diligent one. For every youngster in tobacco country knows the little parasite as a "love vine" said to possess magical powers over matters of the heart.

If you find a love vine, it is said, then you must lay it on a bush and leave it there overnight. If the vine is still alive the next morning, you know that your sweetheart loves you. It is a hardy vine that will survive on almost any living plant. Even the old women look for the love vines, and the discovery of one may bring a secret smile under a broad straw hat, or sometimes a burst of raucous laughter. It is a good time to talk with friends about church, scattered families and old loves.

When the plants are ready for setting into the fields, the farmer rigs his tractor with a water barrel and hitches a two-seat mechanical planter onto the rear. With his children or his neighbors feeding the plants into the planting wheel, he moves slowly down the rows. Carefully, symmetrically—forty-two inches between rows, twenty-two inches between plants—a plow on the planter cuts a furrow into the dark, sandy loam, drops a plant and a spurt of water into the cut, and then squeezes the soil up against the plant to keep it upright. The tractor moves slowly, and most small farmers can cover only one row at a time—one going and one coming and every fifth row left vacant for the sled at harvesttime.

Some of the plants will not live, and the farmer must set new plants to replace them. If there is a good rain soon after the transplanting is completed, the ministers in the little Negro churches will offer a special thanksgiving, and the collection plates will be heavier with silver.

The crop will grow for two months, and for the entire growing season it has to be treated with fungicide and insecticide, and chemicals to control the growth of suckers—damaging shoots that grow from the junction of the leaf stem and the stalk. As the tobacco matures, the blossoms that sprout at the top of the plant must be broken on every stalk so that they will not produce seed and retard the growth of the leaf.

And then, one hot summer day, the farmer looks across his field and sees that the leaves at the bottom of the man-high stalk have faded from green to ripe yellow and it is time for the first priming. Each leaf must be picked at just the right stage of maturity, beginning at the bottom of the stalk and working toward the top. Thus, each field must be primed, or harvested, five, six, even seven times. Each harvest must be strung on sticks and hung in the barn for about three or four days of curing by artificial heat produced by oil or gas burners.

The small, boxlike barns are not so much barns as kilns. The summer temperature in the upper rafters is already intense as the tobacco sticks are passed upward to small boys standing precariously on cross poles. Soon after the barn is packed to the bottom and the door bolted with a wooden peg, the heat inside becomes humanly unbearable. The leaves must be drained of every bit of moisture, leaving them almost crisp enough to crumble between the fingers. The curing process is completed, the farmer's work is almost done, when the dried leaves are stacked and allowed to regain their moisture naturally. But the farmer cannot celebrate his harvest until his crop is auctioned on the warehouse floor.

Of the tillers of the soil everywhere, it is unlikely that any can compare to the American tobacco farmer in ability to build up and then knock down straw men of imagined peril. He has his share and more of real peril. A hailstorm can and frequently does wipe him out. A flash fire in his curing barn can destroy from a third to half his profit. His plant bed might produce mold-infested plants that will not be discovered until too late. Too much rain or too little, an unusual cold snap or prolonged heat wave, any of these can affect the quality of the crop to such an extent that its market value is less than the cost of producing it.

But perhaps because the tobacco farmer is so completely dependent on one crop, because the profit margin is so thin and the crop so small, his burden of imagined peril often becomes heavier than reality. In his anxiety, he can project into a potential crop disaster a three-day rain, a ten-degree drop in temperature, one wilted plant, or a tiny brown spot on a single leaf. A casual remark by an antitobacco congressman can become a threat of immediate abandonment of the government's price-support system by the time word reaches the tobacco fields.

Maybe it has always been this way. If it is worse today than it was ten years ago or fifty years ago, that is pardonable. For hundreds of thousands of tobacco farmers the underlying fear is not for this year's harvest alone. It is the nagging, gnawing knowledge that their days are numbered. They know that they must make the best crop possible this year because next year's crop might be their last one. To know that, the farmer need only look about him.

The nation gets its grain, its beef, its cotton, even its fruits and vegetables from vast farms and ranches and plantations that stretch almost from horizon to horizon, where a moving tractor can shrink from life-size to speck-size without changing rows.

Much of the world's supply of flue-cured tobacco, on the other hand, is produced on family farms, where the tobacco crop covers considerably less ground than a small city block. In North Carolina alone, where more than half of the nation's flue-cured tobacco is grown, the average size of all tobacco allotments is right at three acres. Many farmers own and till more land in other crops. But the number of acres each farmer is allowed to plant in tobacco and the maximum amount of tobacco he is allowed to produce per acre are allotted by the federal goverment.

A man with a fifty-acre tobacco allotment is a rich planter in tobacco country. That is why tobacco is agriculture's last great stronghold of hand labor, the last to resist mechanization, and that is why the average tobacco farmer knows that his days are numbered. The huge machines that rumble across the nation's grain fields and its cotton plantations are a recent and still rare occurrence in the tobacco fields. Except for his tractor and the semi-automated transplanter, the little tobacco farmer still must rely mainly on his strong back and his hands, plus the backs and the hands of his wife and his children, his neighbors and their wives and their children. Many small farmers cannot afford even the tractor. They plow the rows with a mule and set the plants by hand, using a small wooden plug to punch the hole for the plant. The new plant gets its spurt of water from a bucket carried along the rows by a small boy, plus the sweat dripping into the soil from the farmer's chin.

It is not the fault of technology. Rather, it is a matter of economics. With good land, good luck and a good poundage quota, the good four-acre farmer can, with his allotment, produce a crop that will bring a gross return on the market of $1,200 to $1,500 per acre, or a total gross of $5,000 to $6,000 for the year. For a great many farm families it is less.

If he owns the land and farms it himself, he must deduct from his gross the money to buy seed and fertilizer, insecticides and fungicides, gas or oil to heat the curing barn, and gas to run his tractor and his truck. He must maintain and provide for replacement of perhaps $10,000 worth of equipment, including tractor, truck, plows, disks, transplanter and barn furnace. He must pay something for hired labor during the transplanting and the harvesting, unless he has a large family and a work-swapping agreement with his neighbors.

If the farmer is a sharecropper, farming land owned by another man and using equipment provided by another man, he might receive up to half the gross. Of that, his net might be as little as one per cent or as much as twenty-five per cent.

If the farmer is a tenant, he will receive free housing of sorts for twelve months and the minimum wage whenever the owner needs the tenant's back and his hands, usually not more than four months out of the year.

In this kind of economic structure it is little wonder that the market for technology's assembly line is a mighty thin one in tobacco country. The marvel is that so many farmers have been able to survive at all. A great many of them have not survived as productive farmers. In North Carolina alone, 42,000 farms went under during the period from 1959 to 1964. Most of them were small tobacco farms. The attrition is not that rapid now, but it goes on at a steady pace. The little farmer knows that he must get out or get bigger. In either case, it is not much of a choice. A tobacco allotment is highly negotiable. But it cannot be sold or transferred across a county line. Until the federal government abolishes that rule, as it had to do years ago when cotton was caught in the same predicament, the development of large corporate farms capable of operating profitably never will reach its potential. When that day comes, the small farmer will have a real choice. If he is not capable of getting bigger, he will at least be able to get out profitably.

In the meantime, the little farmers either barely hang on or get out the best way they can. Some put their land into the soil bank or turn to raising chickens or to truck farming. Many acres lie fallow, growing nothing but honeysuckle and fishing worms. In 1969, North Carolina farmers held 416,000 acres of tobacco allotment in 115,000 separate allotments; the allotment was not planted on 35,000 acres. Unplanted acreage has been increasing steadily by 5,000 acres a year since 1966.

Some farmers have tried to hold onto their allotment and rent it out to other producers. It worked for a while, returning a net of $200 and $300 an acre in rental. But then the market for rental acreage began dropping. In 1966, a man owning an acreage-poundage quota entitling him to produce four acres of tobacco and market 1,200 pounds per acre could rent his allotment for twenty cents a pound. By 1969, the average rental price had dropped to ten cents a pound, and some allotments were rented for five cents a pound.

Clearly, too many people are trying to squeeze a living out of too little land. Despite the heavy out-migration since the end of World War II, the coastal-plains region still contains the nation's densest farm population. Some people must go, and the landless black knows very well that his is the most tenuous position. There is a touch of irony in that.

One day back in the early fall of 1839, a black slave named Stephen built a little charcoal fire inside the log barn where his master's tobacco crop was curing. History has not recorded the reason for the fire. It might be that Stephen, denied even the dignity of a last name, knew more about tobacco than the masters of his day knew. It is possible that he was knowingly conducting an experiment in the curing process. More likely, Stephen built the fire simply to keep warm, or maybe to cook a piece of pork or a wild rabbit.

Whatever the reason, that little fire in Caswell County, N.C., started the first great revolution in tobacco growing. As the heat mounted inside the curing barn, the landowner, Abisha Slade, discovered that the aroma of the tobacco improved and the color of the big leaves turned to a golden yellow.

By accident or design, a black man had discovered the flue-curing process—that is, curing by artificial heat.

In so doing, he found the key to a kingdom and helped create a way of life, a social order unlike that of any other section of the United States and one that would endure with little change for well over a century.

Tobacco had been grown and marketed successfully in the U.S. for more than 200 years before the flue-curing process was discovered. It is credited with saving the nation's first permanent colony at Jamestown because it gave the settlers a profitable agricultural export. As early as 1618, Jamestown realized a $10,950 return on its tobacco crop. But 200 years later, tobacco was still essentially a Virginia product because the naturally cured leaf of that day did not take well to the soil of other Southern states.

The flue-curing process changed that. Bright Leaf, or flue-cured, tobacco became the dominant variety on the market and, within a few years, the coin of the realm in Virginia and the Carolinas, fully justifying its title, "The Golden Token."

Vast fortunes were made on tobacco. It built cities and roads, hospitals and universities. Merchants and even clergymen were paid in tobacco. It created also a class of yeoman farmers, men whose tiny patch of tobacco gave them the essential freedom, if not the wealth, of the Virginia aristocrats and the delta cotton planters. The tobacco farms were small in comparison with the cotton plantations. But because tobacco was such a demanding crop, it had to have as much or more hand labor than cotton did. And so there developed on the small tobacco farms a structured social order that even the large cotton plantations could not support for long.

The landowner, if he farms more than ten acres, depends on sharecroppers and tenants to produce the crop. Even the sharecroppers, often more prosperous than the small landowners, must count heavily on the labor of dirt-poor blacks, who are paid a modest wage during the brief harvesting season but given little more than free housing the rest of the year. Thus, for hundreds of thousands of families—poor whites as well as blacks—tobacco has offered little more than bare survival in a near-feudal system.

But modern technology is beginning to move into the tobacco fields, to shake the ancient social order. One agent of this social revolution is a huge, Rube Goldberg-like contraption called a tobacco harvester. It has been fifteen years in the making, and although it is still not widely used, the day is not far off when hundreds of them will rumble through the tobacco fields, displacing tens of thousands of sun-scorched laborers and marginal farmers.

The trend toward large corporate farms is clearly evident. It requires no great imagination to foresee the day, maybe five or ten years from now, when a relatively few such farms will grow all the flue-cured tobacco the market demands—plant it, transplant it, harvest it, cure it and market it with machines instead of men.

Already technology and the nation's economy have started a massive upheaval in the life of the region. In 1950, when tobacco was cultivated almost entirely by hand, twenty-five workers were needed to grow twenty-five acres of tobacco. Today, with only scattered adoption of partial mechanization and chemical methods, the average manpower requirement for the same twenty-five acres is about twenty workers. Widespread use of the new tobacco harvester alone probably will bring the figure down to four workers for every twenty-five acres.

For a great many tobacco farmers it does not really matter whether the upheaval is completed in one season or stretched out over five seasons, even a decade. These are the small farmers, mostly black tenants and sharecroppers, who have precious little hope of surviving the social revolution no matter how gradually it develops. Tens of thousands of them are leaving the tobacco fields every year, unable to survive on the tenant's share of a five-acre patch or less.

Leaving the farm is not an easy thing to do. The farm is home, even when home is a shack owned by the man up the road. It is a nail beside the kitchen door where the hat has been hung for thirty years. It is the old cane-bottomed chair under the shade tree, where ice water tastes so good at the end of a summer day. It is the smell of manure and old harness leather, and the memory of young love carved on the barn door: ABS & JT AUG 1930. It is the church and the graveyard, where parents and brothers and sisters and babies are buried. It is the debt still owed to the bank or the store or the landlord—a debt that never seems to go away no matter how good the crop is.

It is hard to leave the farm because there never is a good time to leave it. In winter, there is not even enough money to buy food, and so it is better to stay where you can get food on credit until the crop is sold next year. In spring and summer, there is a crop in the ground; a man cannot leave a crop to rot in the fields. In the fall, when the crop is harvested and sold and there is a little money, there is still the debt. Always there is the debt.

But the farmer's sons do not owe the debt. Thousands of them leave the day they graduate from high school. Some must stay until the tobacco is barned because there is no one else to do it. Others must wait until the crop is sold and there is money to buy a ticket north. Very few of them old enough to leave will stay beyond harvesttime. By September or October, when the last of the crop is harvested in North Carolina, probably ninety per cent of all the region's black highschool graduates are gone. This continuing, staggering exodus from the farms is heaviest in the summer months because most of today's migrants are the youngsters.

On the last day of May in 1969, thousands of these youngsters from hundreds of schools throughout the 600-mile length of the region were visiting or planning to visit train stations and bus stations.

They were youngsters like Donnie Gibson—black and poor, for the most part; high-school graduates and some dropouts; the sons and daughters of tenant farmers and sharecroppers, small landowners, day laborers, and even some schoolteachers. They had been visiting the stations singly and in groups for weeks. Not all of them would leave at the same time. Many were checking schedules and prices, buying tickets, or picking up tickets purchased on prepayment orders in New York— or Philadelphia or one of a dozen other places from Washington north—and sent south as graduation presents.

Chapter Seven

THE STATION

The Seaboard Coast Line station in Kingstree is much like railroad stations in small towns anywhere in the nation except that it is cleaner and, at certain times of the year, busier.

For reasons that might go back a decade and a half, to the time when Williamsburg County remodeled its ante-bellum courthouse into a gleaming and rather aseptic monument to the region's rich history, the train station is local headquarters for that little band of down-home philosophers characteristic of almost every county seat in the rural South. In others towns, this mixed brigade of the elders and the unemployed—sometimes all white, sometimes all black, often tolerably integrated—gravitates naturally toward the county courthouse or the benches around a local monument to the Civil War. But in Kingstree, the bronze soldiers and granite shafts are benchless, and the alabaster elegance of the courthouse is unspoiled by the stains of tobacco juice and the remains of dead cigarettes.

Kingstree philosophers—almost all black—gather instead at the train station, which sits roughly in the middle of the four-block-long business district, where the tracks bisect Main Street into an uptown section on the east and the beginning of the black section on the west.

Thus located, the station is convenient to those who must walk. There is nearby free parking for those who can afford cars, provided the owners do not dally too long in discussions about the weather, the crop conditions, the comings and goings of friends and relatives and the sad state of local employment. The discussion groups usually are small and short-lived, because the philosophers are members of a fluid club. They do not come into town every day, and there are other stops to make.

Not counting the freights, which do not create much of a stir, Kingstree gets only four passenger trains a day, and two of them do not always stop. It is the Gulf Coast Special that carries almost all of the traffic. The southbound train stops at 1:20 in the afternoon, the northbound train at 2:40 in the afternoon. The Everglades, running between New York and Jacksonville, Florida, comes through at 8:53 P.M., southbound, and at 5:40 A.M., heading north. They do not have much business at Kingstree, and the Champion, the crack train carrying the carriage trade between Saint Petersburg and New York, almost never stops, because it is mostly Pullman traffic.

So, on many days of the year, the nontravelers are the major source of movement around the station; and the railroad, in the person of its local agent, maintains a tolerant attitude as long as the club meets alfresco. Agent E. B. Bailey is a man of generous girth and nature. But he is a believer in functional cleanliness and efficiency, and he insists—rightly, it can be argued—that the waiting room is there for the benefit of ticket holders. Inside, the station is kept cool in summer and warm in winter, and covered regularly with a fresh coat of paint, even if it must be the bilious gray dictated by railroad tradition.

Outside, Bailey's tolerance of nontravelers is readily apparent. From the overhang of the red tile roof down to the pavement, the station walls are about ninety per cent clean white stucco. But at knee height, there is a line of dirt and scuff marks running around the building. In good weather, the men of the community gather around the freight wagons in the yard. When it is raining or when the sun is bouncing heat waves off the pavement, the men retreat to the cover of the overhang and stand on one foot, storklike, with the other braced against the wall of the station.

On the hot Saturday morning that Donnie and Jessie and Julia Gibson arrived at the station, Agent Bailey was about as near as he ever comes to being fretful. Holidays and graduations are trying times for railroad- and bus-station agents throughout the rural coastal-plains region of the South.

Jessie parked the car, and then they went up the street to cash Renea's money order and linger over a sandwich and a soda. When they returned to the station, just after noon, they were surprised at the size of the crowd that had gathered.

When they first arrived, they had noticed the usual small clusters of people. But now the little yard between the station and Main Street was jammed with people and suitcases. It was hot—Donnie guessed it must have been in the high nineties—and there was little movement among the crowd, except when someone jockeyed for a spot in the shade next to the building. Mostly, they stood silently beside their bags or talked sparingly in family groups.

The one person who seemed to be doing any great amount of moving was Rufus Miller, a roving photographer who has worked the train station at selected times of the year for at least a decade. He lent a dash of festive flavor to the scene with his Polaroid camera and his chant.

"Just sixty seconds," Miller said over and over as he moved slowly but constantly through the crowd. "Just sixty seconds. That's all it takes. Take a little bit of Kingstree with you so you'll feel like comin' back. Just sixty seconds."

Julia and Donnie went inside to get the ticket, joining a short line at the ticket window. They noticed that the little waiting room was full. Actually, half of it was full; the other half had been blocked off with a fresh coat of paint.

It was cool inside, but Agent Bailey was having some trouble keeping it that way. "Please close the door," he called out repeatedly. "We're trying to keep it cool in here."

Julia was ahead of Donnie in the line, and when the youngster in front of her got his ticket and turned to leave, Julia moved up to the wire-mesh window to order Donnie's ticket.

"All right?" the agent said.

"A ticket to Brooklyn, New York, please."

"All right. One way?"

"Yessir. One way," Julia said.

The agent lifted a yellow ticket out of a cubbyhole on

his right and quickly ran it through the old Aurora dater on the counter, pulling the ticket through with his left hand and rapidly stamping it four times with the heel of his right fist. He ripped off the bottom section of the ticket, dropped it into his receipts drawer and slipped the three remaining portions into a bright orange-and-white envelope decorated with two palm trees, a sleek passenger train and the letters *S C L* in large black print at the top. Across the bottom was printed "Seaboard Coast Line Railroad."

"One way to New York," the agent said, sliding the envelope through the window toward Julia. "That'll be twenty-eight seventy-four."

Donnie had reached for his burglarproof wallet while the agent was making out the ticket and then remembered that he had put the cash from the money order into his shirt pocket. "Not such a good beginning on looking out for my money," he thought, as he pushed a twenty and a ten across the counter.

"Twenty-eight seventy-four out of thirty," Bailey said, counting out the change. "Thank you, and the train leaves at 2:40."

Donnie put the silver into his pocket. The dollar bill and the five he still had went into the wallet. Six dollars and something. That was not much, but he reckoned he wouldn't need much. There would have been more, counting all the money the neighbors had given him for graduation—maybe ten or twelve dollars—and the four dollars he had earned working Mr. Canty's tobacco last week. He had given all of it to Julia except one dollar, and he had blown that on sodas and candy the last week of school.

Julia had picked up the ticket envelope, and now she handed it to Donnie. "Now you take good care of this ticket," she said. "You lose it and they'll put you off the train."

Outside, the two of them went back to the car, where Jessie was waiting with the bags. Donnie felt the need to end it quickly, and he started to say something but Julia cut him short.

"Well, you take care of yourself now," Julia said, "and call every chance you get."

It was done, and Donnie turned quickly, without saying anything, and headed back through the crowd. He thought there might be a shady spot left over at the side of the building, the track side, next to the freight platform.

Jessie carried one of the bags and then left to do some shopping uptown. Julia sat in the car fanning herself and trying not to think of anything. She would not leave the car until after the train had pulled out—nearly two hours later.

Chapter Eight
CREAM OF THE CROP

Virgil Dimery is Kingstree's leading black activist, perhaps its leading black citizen as well. As he looked at the crowd at the Kingstree station that Saturday, he wondered, for what must have been the thousandth time, when it would ever end. When in God's name would it end?

It had been going on now, this annual exodus, for at least twenty years. He knew it went back that far, maybe farther. Every year it was the same thing. We raise our kids and put them through high school and for what? To pack their bags and tell them good-by. We see them again on holidays or at next year's graduation, when they come down to pick up somebody else in the family and take them North. And sometimes, Dimery knew, they were not seen again until they came home in a shipping box. He remembered Calvin Barr's boy Omega and Willie Johnson's youngest boy, Sammie Joe.

Omega Barr couldn't find any steady work, and when Calvin sold his little tobacco crop in the fall of 1964, Omega had gone up to the train station and bought a ticket for Philadelphia because an uncle had told him there was work there. Omega rented a room and got a job right away in construction. But he didn't like it. He saved a little money, and by the time he came home to visit at Easter in 1967, he had decided to come back and try farming again. His daddy was getting too old to handle the acre of tobacco. He had arthritis real bad and just couldn't follow the plow any more. Calvin and Lessie Barr wanted their son to come back and take over the farm, and Omega figured he might be able to get some equipment and make a go of it. They talked it over at Easter, and when Omega left to go back to Philadelphia he had made up his mind.

"Don't you worry none, Mama," he told Lessie. "I'm coming back in September and I'm gonna stay." He kissed her on the cheek, and she stood there on the porch wondering why he had to go back at all.

Then one night about six weeks later, Lessie was midwifing the birth of her fourth great-grandbaby when the telephone rang. Her daughter Blanche answered the telephone because Lessie's granddaughter Elizabeth was having a hard delivery. The labor had started twelve hours earlier, and it was just now about to end.

Lessie heard the telephone ring in the next room and did not give it much mind. Maybe a minute later, she heard Blanche scream.

"What is it?" Lessie called to her daughter. "What is it?"

"Oh, Mama," Blanche said, "Omega's been stabbed. 'Mega's dead."

Lessie had stood up, holding onto the bedpost. Now she, too, screamed, and fell back onto the foot of the bed. Her second scream was interrupted by her granddaughter's cry for help, and Lessie knew that life must be celebrated before death.

She pulled the baby into the world and swabbed out his mouth so he would not choke. But she was too tired, too distraught, to cut the umbilical cord. She looked about her for the towels to wrap the baby in and realized that she had forgot to bring them in and that she needed help. She called to one of her grandsons in the next room and told him to run next door and get Willie Mae Tisdale. "And tell her to bring something to wrap the baby in," she said.

Lessie sat numbly on the side of the bed, holding

her new great-grandson and mourning her dead son. Blanche told her all she knew about Omega's death. He had come home from work and had been stabbed by a man hiding in the shadows of the hallway at his apartment house.

When Mrs. Tisdale arrived, Lessie passed the baby to her and went to the kitchen to wash up. Then she sat at the kitchen table and cried and prayed: "Lord, have mercy. Lord. Do, Lord, have mercy."

Virgil Dimery buried Omega in May, and a year later he buried Sammie Joe Johnson, whose daddy lives just down the street from the funeral home. Dimery never did hear how Sammie Joe was killed. Sammie Joe's parents didn't know much about it either, except that Sammie Joe was shot in a bar in Brooklyn, New York.

Virgil remembered those two and many others. Dimery and Rogers Funeral Home is the largest funeral home for blacks in Kingstree, and a good portion of its business, maybe twenty-five or thirty funerals a year, is ship-in business. The other two places get some ship-ins, too. The bodies for Kingstree and surrounding small towns come into the Kingstree station at the rate of 300 or so a year. Last weekend alone, there had been eight shipped in, mostly from New York and Newark and Philadelphia and Rochester, New York.

Somewhere, Dimery had heard or seen a figure on Rochester a couple of years ago. Something like 8,000 people in the city of Rochester had come originally from Williamsburg County, South Carolina. Funny thing about Rochester. He had tried to check into it one time to see how it had started. Best he could figure it out, it was two brothers named Wallace. They had gone to Rochester sometime in the late forties. They got pretty good jobs, and after that it was the same thing that happens in other cities: come back and get a brother or a sister or a cousin, and eventually, as the parents get older or need medical care, come back and get the parents; the next thing you know, the neighbors are going up there.

"My God," he thought. "We're being bled dry here, and it don't seem to be anything we can do about it. Not just this county of Williamsburg. Every county around here. Up in North Carolina, too. And Georgia. All the farming country." That was the trouble. It was farming country. Little farms, where a man was lucky just to be able to hang on. And that wouldn't last long. Tobacco was shot, and tobacco is what kept the little farms going. Jobs in industry were pitifully few, and most of them were for the whites. All of them had been for whites until three or four years ago, when colored people started putting some pressure on and asking questions in Washington.

The real tragedy of it, Virgil knew, was the kids, the high-school graduates. The old folks, most of them, could hang on. They never had had anything anyway, and they had learned to live with it. But these kids, they're the cream of the crop. A high-school diploma wasn't much of an education in Williamsburg County, for whites or blacks. Hell, anybody in his right mind and honest enough to admit it knew that. All you had to do was look at the draft figures. Eighty-six per cent of the black kids failed the draft tests and forty-five per cent of the whites. There were some smart ones, of course. But Dimery knew that for many black kids, a high-school education was the equivalent of a sixth- or seventh- or eighth-grade education. He could back that up with the results of college-entrance tests. But that wasn't the fault of the kids. They were still the cream of the crop. They'd had the grit to stick it out to graduation, many times in spite of circumstances that made it a whole lot easier to quit.

So here it was graduation time again, and Dimery would not have had to come to the train station to know what was happening. He had brought a man up to put him on the train and almost wished he hadn't. Maybe he would not have thought about it. No, that was not right. He had been thinking about it all week. They had been coming into his office all week—sometimes ten or fifteen a day—looking for work or advice.

What could they do? Where should they go?

Dimery did not know the answers. But it did not matter that he could not advise them. They would do what they had to do. They would leave.

Graduation at the county's twelve high schools—five white and seven Negro—had started Wednesday night, the last week in May. By Saturday, when they were finished, the schools had turned out 707 graduates. Two hundred and twenty of the graduates were white, 487 black. The lucky ones would go on to college—probably thirty per cent of the whites and maybe ten per cent of the blacks. But that still left around 600 graduates, and not much more than four times that many people were on a full-time payroll in the whole county. As for jobs available, well, the man up at the state employment service had 2,100 applications on file for jobs in Baxter Laboratories, biggest single employer in the county. Kingstree Manufacturing had 500 to 600 on file. Maybe ten or fifteen per cent of the graduates would find a job around here in a three- or four-county area. The rest would be gone by the end of the summer. Most of them would be gone in three weeks. The others would have to wait and leave after the tobacco was in the barns in July, or maybe stay until it was sold a few weeks later, because there would be no ticket money before then.

Chapter Nine
A BUSY DAY

Rounding the corner of the station, Donnie heard the radio first and then saw Harim Morant. Right away, he realized he had left his own radio at home.

"Hey, man," Donnie said, slapping Harim on the shoulder. "You leaving, too?"

"Yep, I'm gonna take me a little vacation," Harim said. "Might even get me a job."

At twenty and stretching more than six feet, Harim was about the oldest and the tallest, and maybe the friendliest, member of Donnie's class of eighty-three at Williamsburg County Training School. He never took much of anything seriously. Donnie liked him, and al-

A Busy Day

ready his spirits were better than they had been in days. Harim had never been to New York before either, never had ridden a train before, and they both were going to Brooklyn. They made a pact that whoever got on board first would save the other one a seat, and then they settled down with Harim's radio to wait for the train.

It was too hot to stir around much, but now and then Donnie saw faces in the crowd that he recognized. One was Eddie Mae Dotts, who was in his class. Her cousin in the Bronx had sent her the money for the ticket, and Eddie Mae was going to live with her until fall. By then, she hoped to be enrolled in a nursing course that her cousin had told her about. Then there was Harim's friend, a girl named Rosetta McGill, and Donnie saw Viola Williams. Both of them were going to New York, also.

Inside the station, Agent Bailey began counting up the day's receipts around two o'clock, soon after the mail and the few passengers had been cleared from the southbound train. It was a short one. The big southbound traffic had been earlier in the week—people coming down for graduations—and some of the trains had run in two sections, one an hour behind the other. Today, there was the normal one, and it had pulled out at 1:20, just about the time Number 76 was rolling into Charleston on the northbound run. They would be passing right about now, down the line near Monks Corner, unless Number 76 was running late. This time of the year that was likely, Agent Bailey knew.

Traffic memos and advisories had been going up and down the lines of the Seaboard for weeks, as they always do before holidays and graduations, so Number 76 would be pulling additional equipment today—six to eight coaches instead of the usual two or three. There were six additional coaches up the line at Florence to be hooked on if the traffic justified it.

Agent Bailey knew, as he had known all along, that the extra coaches waiting in Florence would be justified. Maybe not all of them would have to be put into service this weekend, but two or three would have to be hooked on. He had predicted that this first weekend would be comparatively light, that the biggest loadings would come the next weekend and the one after that. He had been at Kingstree fifteen years, and he had learned to gauge the traffic patterns pretty accurately.

Normally, Number 76 rolls into Kingstree pulling two or three coaches and a Pullman. Day in and day out the coaches are seldom full. They might have thirty to fifty passengers totally, against a capacity of fifty to sixty passengers per coach. But the traffic picks up considerably at holidays, and especially at graduation time each year. It has been that way for quite some time, although Bailey has noticed what seems to be a very slight lessening of the exodus in the past three or four years.

Just a few years ago, there were many June days when the Kingstree station alone would board up to 300 northbound passengers, as many as the train had on it when it pulled into the station. There were even times when Number 76 left Kingstree with passengers standing in the baggage cars. The railroad was severely criticized for that, and they don't allow it any more. But the passengers wanted to go. They had bought their tickets, and so it was allowed several times when the exodus had been greater than the railroad had anticipated.

Today and for the next two or three Saturdays—for some reason the youngsters traveled mostly on Saturdays, maybe because they had to arrive at their destination on the weekend when someone would be off work to meet them—Number 76 would leave Kingstree with standing room only. By the end of June, if past experience held true, the Kingstree station would have boarded from 750 to 1,000 passengers headed North, not counting children under six, who travel free. Not all of them would be fresh migrants from this year's class. Some would be adults who had left in previous years and come back for graduation or to pick up small children who had been staying with grandparents through the school year.

Throughout the coastal-plains region there are tens of thousands of such youngsters—so many, in fact, that the local school boards have recently begun to count them and, in some areas, impose tuition charges.

In Williamsburg County alone, the school superintendent has estimated that twenty per cent of the entire county's school population, probably a quarter or more of the black school population, is composed of youngsters whose parents live outside the state—in most cases, somewhere in the urban areas from Washington, D.C. to New York State. This does not take into account perhaps an equal number who have not yet reached school age. In the Gibson family, for example, of the six children with out-of-state parents, three are of preschool age. The three oldest live with their grandparents year-round. The others shuttle back and forth between Williamsburg County and Brooklyn, spending most of the year in the South and going to Brooklyn for visits that might last from one to three months.

In Warren County, N.C., the school board surveyed the school population in the spring of 1969 before imposing a tuition fee on nonresident students beginning the following fall. The survey showed that nearly eight per cent of the total school population and more than twelve per cent of the Negro school population were children whose parents lived outside the county—outside the state in all but a few cases. One-third of the nonresident students did not know the whereabouts of one or the other parent; one-tenth did not know where either parent lived at the time of the survey.

Many of these youngsters are the children of unmarried mothers who work and have no way to care for the small children. Others live in the South for economic reasons. Still others are sent back home for their education because their parents say they do not want their children attending the urban schools. These parents are not deluded by the academic differences in rural and urban schools. But they are less concerned about the quality of instruction than they are about the degree of social pressures on youngsters in urban ghetto schools.

Bailey totted up his final count of ticket sales just before 2:30. By now almost everyone who was going had bought a ticket. The latecomers could purchase on board from the conductor, as everyone did in the smaller towns.

It had been a busy day. Two to Washington, four to Baltimore, eight to Philadelphia, eight to Newark and thirty-six to New York City. None to Rochester, but then Rochester people were riding the buses lately, for the most part. Altogether that made fifty-eight going North. Bailey had been slightly off. Earlier in the week he had guessed that this first weekend would run somewhere between forty and fifty. But he would learn later that he had been right on his estimate of the June total. Kingstree boardings averaged better than one hundred for each of the following three Saturdays, not counting the twenty to forty passengers who boarded Number 76 on most weekdays.

Chapter Ten

THE CHICKENBONE SPECIAL

If on a clear day you stand alongside the tracks at the station in Kingstree and look south, you can see the train coming from six miles away.

At night, when the Champion or the Everglades comes through, you can see the headlight from twenty miles away, when it tops a little hill at Saint Stephen, beyond the Santee River swamp. But in Kingstree almost nobody takes the Everglades, and the Champion is for people who can afford sleepers and compartments, and who make reservations months ahead. The people who ride the train out of Kingstree sleep at home and ride coaches when they take a train; so they take the word of those who have seen the train by night and marvel instead at the six-mile sighting in daylight.

But even then, to see the train you have to stand close to the track and watch carefully, for the engine is visible first as only a tiny flash, then another and another as the beam of the revolving headlight probes and pierces and then falls away from the shimmering heat waves rising above the railroad bed. Soon after the first sighting, you momentarily lose the train when it dips into a swampy area. But seconds later, when it has risen to level ground again, the beam is more constant. The speck of light is now a beacon surrounded by a dark blur, which becomes recognizable as the nose of a train rushing toward the station at eighty miles an hour and then seventy, sixty, fifty—until it is so close you can hear the sound of the air horn and feel on the track under your feet the rumble of the wheels.

The crowd in the station yard hears the blast of the horn and watches the mechanical arms drop across Main Street to stop traffic across the tracks, and its mood changes. The youngsters who have been noisy suddenly become quiet, and old people who have been quiet suddenly feel the need to talk. Portable radios are clicked off. Bags are lifted. Hands are held and shaken. Cheeks and lips are kissed and clung to. Eyes mist. Faces smile. People say good-by, take care and write me or call me; be a good boy, be a good girl, stay out of trouble.

The crowd is packed close against the tracks when the engine rolls by and delivers the appropriate car to the loading area. The symphony of throbbing Diesels and the creaking, jolting brake of first one car and then another now swell the voices beside the train. Rufus Miller packs his camera into his shoulder case, for he knows there will be no customer arriving on a northbound train.

Along Main Street, people stand under awnings and look at the train and, in their mind, beyond it—to where it is going and where it has come from. Motorists sit in their cars damning the train and the people who make it necessary for the train to stop and block traffic in the heat of the day. But some of them envy the boarding passengers. For a few moments—a few angry, wistful moments—this unthinking machine stops the life of the town, pulls dreams and curses out of the people, moves on to the next town. And when it is gone, with its noise and its nuisance and its passengers looking out the windows, the town seems strangely quiet for a little while.

Donnie Gibson was among the last passengers to board, but all the Kingstree passengers were boarding a single coach and Donnie knew Harim would save him a seat.

As it turned out, Harim had saved three extra seats, all of them in the first two rows at the front of the car. They were the kind that face one another, and as Donnie put his bags into the rack overhead he noticed that Viola and Rosetta were in the seats facing his and Harim's.

Donnie sat down and then remembered that he

would have to have his ticket ready when the conductor came through. He pulled the ticket envelope out of his rear pants pocket, opened the flap to make sure the ticket was still inside, and then noticed some printing on the back side of the envelope under a notice that said "Your Trip."

"You are about to take a trip by train—the most dependable, carefree, comfortable form of travel known," Donnie read.

"Seaboard Coast Line wishes you a pleasant trip.

"Should it become necessary to change your plans, please notify your Ticket Agent or nearest Seaboard Coast Line Office as soon as possible.

"Due to the great demand at certain seasons of the year, reservations for your return trip should be arranged as early as possible.

"Whenever you travel, it is a pleasure for us to serve you."

Seaboard does indeed try to serve its passengers. Some employees say that Seaboard is the only railroad in the country any more that gives a damn about passenger business, and a Florida–to–New York trip on the Champion, say, or the Silver Meteor or the Silver Star, can be downright enjoyable to a man who can afford a sleeper and who is in no great hurry to get there. The company does what it can to make even coach travel comfortable. The cars are air-conditioned, and they are precooled for hours before they are put into service so that the passengers do not have to wait out the heat while the compressors and the Freon perform their engineering marvel over the elements. Normally, the coaches are clean, the rest rooms are clean, and the water fountains dispense cold water.

So it is not altogether Seaboard's fault that the Gulf Coast Special at certain times of the year is considerably less than "the most dependable, carefree, comfortable form of travel known."

The company maintains enough modern equipment to handle the normal daily passenger traffic in reasonable comfort. To meet the unusual demands of graduations and some holidays along its tracks, though, the railroad must call into service some ancient coaches that spend much of the year growing old gracefully on some peaceful siding. The aged ones respond with creaking and groaning and, almost always, a balky cooling system.

The car assigned to the Kingstree passengers was just such an elder citizen, and the passengers needed only a few minutes to discover that fact. They were hot when they boarded from the sun-baked station yard. Within minutes after the train pulled out they were sweltering. The air-conditioning system was not working on this coach, or on another one up front. The conductor said that mechanics were waiting in Florence, and would try to fix it when the train stopped there in about half an hour.

The Kingstree passengers found their own solution. The late boarders had spilled over into the coach behind to find seats and discovered that it was not only air-conditioned but also empty. Those jubilant words were passed quickly to the main Kingstree group, and some of the mothers with young children moved. But the main body of teen-agers decided to stay in the hot coach, partly through camaraderie and partly because of the warning issued loudly by a veteran of previous trips on the train.

"Forget it, man," he said to everybody and nobody in particular. "You better stay where you are. You get in that air-conditioned car and you gonna freeze all night long. It don't make no difference whether you hot all day or freezing all night. That's this old 'Chickenbone Special' for you."

He had to be a veteran, because only the veterans and train crewmen from New York to Jacksonville know the Gulf Coast Special by its nickname.

The name is thought to have originated back in the late fifties among a group of black graduate students at Temple University in Philadelphia. Over beer one night, reminiscing about life in the Carolinas, they discovered that most if them had come north at one time or another on the same train. Further, they remembered the lunches packed by anxious mothers for sons and daughters who could not afford the prices charged on railroad dining cars. Invariably, those lunches contained at least one piece of fried chicken, as they still do —a fact that can be verified by an inspection of one of the coaches after it has disgorged its passengers at New York's Penn Station.

Technically, the nickname is no longer correct in that it is still used in the singular. The name was coined in the days when there was only one Chickenbone Special—the Seaboard Air Line Railroad's once-a-day whistle-stopper from Tampa to New York City. The Atlantic Coast Line Railroad had its equivalent train—

the Palmland—which made a daily run from Florida to New York on tracks roughly paralleling the Seaboard tracks north into Richmond and generally fifty to a hundred miles inland from the Seaboard tracks.

Thus when the Seaboard and the Atlantic Coast merged into the Seaboard Coast Line several years ago, there were suddenly two Chickenbone Specials. But the company has taken an incidental step toward remedying this problem of a singular name for a plural train. Because of schedule changes, two trains, Number 10 and Number 76 (the Gulf Coast Special), merge in Richmond shortly after 10:00 every night; so the Chickenbone Special is in fact one train when it rolls across the Potomac River about 1:00 A.M. into the southern tip of the nation's East Coast urban area.

Even with the string of cars it pulls into Washington on its busiest days, the Chickenbone Special is not much of a train any more, in comparison with what it once was.

In their heyday, the two trains thrived on the rich vacation traffic between New York and Miami, and the passengers were undoubtedly the kind who appreciate little niceties like the historical plaques screwed into the walls of the coaches—descriptions of places like Mary Washington House, where George Washington's mother was a gracious hostess at lawn parties and served wine and cake in the "Best Room." But time and the airplane have wrought some noticeable changes in railroad passenger service. Neither 10 nor 76 touches Miami any more. Number 76 makes up in Tampa at 10:30 every night and heads north toward Jacksonville on its 1,259-mile run to New York City. But there are so few passengers boarding between Tampa and Jacksonville that the railroad has petitioned the government for permission to discontinue that leg of the trip. The Jacksonville-Charleston leg might also become an eventual casualty, since the train does not begin to pick up any appreciable number of passengers until it crosses Georgia into South Carolina.

Number 10, the Palmland, begins in Columbia, S.C., nowadays, and pulls out at 1:10 in the afternoon, just about an hour after Number 76 enters South Carolina at Hardeeville. Typically, it pulls about two coaches on most of its daily runs, the same number as the Gulf Coast Special. At holidays and graduation time, it increases the load to five, six or seven coaches, usually slightly less than the Gulf Coast Special.

Almost all the seats in the two trains are filled somewhere in North Carolina or South Carolina. By the time the trains cross into Virginia—Number 76 near Emporia and Number 10 south of LaCross—the boardings have fallen off to almost nothing.

Some measure of the Chickenbone Special's role in the nation's rural-to-urban migration problem—especially as that problem affects the East Coast—can be gauged by simple arithmetic.

Take the six weeks immediately following the first Saturday in June, for example. On at least three days out of each of those six weeks the two trains pull into Richmond with probably fourteen coaches between them. Each of those coaches is loaded with fifty to sixty persons, or, roughly, 700 souls if you take the low figure as an average. That comes to 2,100 passengers per week, not counting the less busy weekdays. For the six-week period, then, these two trains alone haul something like 12,600 people out of the rural Southeast and into the urban Northeast. Most of them come from the Carolinas, with a smattering from Georgia, and almost all of them are deposited in the Washington-Baltimore area or the Philadelphia–New York City area.

Again, this does not count the weekday traffic; nor does it count the children under six who travel free or the thousands of others who leave by car. Some high-school parking lots are often half filled at graduation with cars bearing the license plates of Northern states—cars in which, as a perceptive Southern lady once noted, "four come down and six go back."

It does not count the hundreds of small towns—and even some small cities—not served by railroad passenger service. At their busiest, the two Seaboard trains touch only fifty-four towns or cities in the Carolinas. In scores of others it is the local Greyhound or Trailways bus that moves the migrant North.

The trains do not provide even the slightest clue to the number of white people migrating out of the region. The people on board are a diverse lot in some ways—youngsters leaving permanently or only for a summer visit or summer work; older people (almost all of them women, seldom adult males) who left the region years ago and are now returning from a visit; a great many small children going North for a visit with their parents. But the faces on board the coaches are uniformly of one color, varying only in shade.

The genteel rich returning from a Miami vacation and the upper-middle-class Southerner bound for a visit with Aunt Sally in Richmond have forsaken the train for the airplane. Those still old-fashioned enough or weak-stomached enough to stick with the trains do not ride coach class.

The coaches, like some of the South's once stately old manor houses, now belong to the former field hands—the sons and daughters of the tobacco fields, dark as the soil and rich only in the pride and hope that lead them ultimately to a ticket counter. The young ones have been educated for jobs that do not exist. The old ones have been forced off tenant farms that cannot support them and into a small-town Southern economy that cannot or will not absorb them except as welfare cases or in the pitifully few and mostly second-rate jobs available. Often they board with little more than the clothes on their backs, the paper bag of fried chicken, and an abiding faith that everything will be all right once they get North to where the jobs are.

For those who find later that the city also cannot absorb them, there is some small solace in the knowledge that welfare in the city is better than welfare in the South.

Behind them is the near-certainty of nothing. Ahead, the nothing is at least still a gamble.

Chapter Eleven
THE FANTASTIC FOUR

Amos Jones sat in his car at the railroad crossing and watched the train pull out of the station yard toward Florence and Washington, and toward Rochester, N.Y., and he was sorry he was not on board. He had planned to be on the train this first Saturday after graduation. But now he would have to wait around for another week to help with the tobacco, to earn some money. And he probably would be riding the bus instead of the train because the bus ticket is cheaper.

Amos and the others—Willie Chandler, James McClary and Ernest Tisdale—had planned to go to Rochester together, just as they had done everything else together for two years. They had talked about it constantly since last fall, when Amos came back home to recount his tales of life in the city.

Amos had spent the summer in Rochester, working at the garage where his brother Herman worked. He had earned enough money to buy a '64 Falcon, and he had had one hell of a time. He had even dated a white girl; and, man, there was more where that came from.

Rochester was jobs and good money. It was the drag strip. It was the Mister Wonderful Club and the Fifty Acres Club, and it was girls—girls everywhere, girls who went to the clubs by themselves and did not mind

The Chickenbone Special

if you asked them to dance and did not mind what color your skin was if you knew how to dance and how to treat a woman.

Rochester was the stuff of dreams in the long winter nights of the senior year, because Amos and his friends did not call themselves the "Fantastic Four" for nothing. They knew how to dance and they knew how to treat a woman. Some guys drove fast cars and wore slick clothes and raised a lot of hell. The Fantastic Four didn't drink because they didn't have the time or the money to drink, and they didn't need to drink. They didn't race because they didn't want any cops watching them every time they parked on a country lane. The Fantastic Four had other things to do. Like Amos told that cat one night at Duffy's Garage when the guy pulled up in his brother's fancy car looking for a race: "Man, you tear up your car and we'll tear up the pussy."

Now school was out, and the Fantastic Four was splitting up. Too many things had gone wrong. Willie Chandler was going. He was leaving Monday. James McClary had failed a course his senior year, and he was going to have to stay around all summer going to school to make it up before he could get his diploma. Ernest had decided to go to Florida because he had a job down there where his brother worked, and he didn't have a sure job in Rochester. Amos was broke because he had had bad luck with a girl.

One day just before school was out, in 1968, Willie had told Amos about this girl who really wanted to go out with Amos.

"Yeah? How you know that?" Amos asked.

The Fantastic Four

"She told me so," Willie said. "She says she wants to give you some pussy. See how good you are."

"Okay. You tell her we'll get together."

Amos's chance came a few days later, when his school bus would not start for the morning run. He reported it and arranged for Willie to make the double run in his bus that afternoon while Amos's bus was in the garage.

At lunchtime that day, Amos guided the girl into a quiet corner. "Willie's been telling me you're kinda curious about me," he said.

"He tell you that?"

"He sure did," Amos said. "You still curious?"

"I might be. You never can tell."

Amos was cool when he put the question to her, trying to let her know that he really did not care what her answer was. "You want to make my bus run with me today?"

"Sure," she said. "Why not?"

Amos explained about the double run. When school was out, she was supposed to mix in with the kids on Willie's bus without letting the principal see her. She and Amos would ride with Willie on his run and then make Amos's run. At the end of the second run, they would have the bus to themselves except for Willie up front driving. Amos would take her home later.

When the second run was completed, Amos turned the wheel over to Willie, and then he and the girl went to the long back seat.

"You up to it?" he asked her.

"Oh, I don't know," she said. "I ain't even sure I know what you talking about."

They played on the seat for a while, and pretty soon Amos knew that it was going to be all right.

"I'm going up to the front to put on some protection," he told her. "When I get back, you be ready."

When Amos returned to the back of the bus, the girl was lying on the seat with her eyes closed. Amos did not see her underwear lying anywhere nearby.

"I thought you were gonna get ready," he said.

"If you want it, you gonna have to do it all yourself," she said.

"Huh uh," he told her. "You gonna help me do it."

She helped him, and later they borrowed Willie's comb for her, and Amos took her home.

He did not see her again until school started in the fall of 1969. He was not really interested enough to give her more than a passing nod when he saw her on the school grounds or in a hallway.

Then in February, he was called to the principal's office. The girl had got pregnant just after school started, and she must have told the principal the name of every boy in school that she had had anything to do with.

"Did you have sex relations with this girl on the school grounds?" the principal asked Amos.

"No sir," Amos said.

"Let me put it this way. Did you have sex relations with this girl on school property during school hours?" the principal asked. This time he emphasized the word *property*.

Amos knew then that the girl must have talked. He knew also that there was no point in lying. He had told the truth when he denied having relations with the girl on the school grounds. But he knew that the bus was considered school property, and he knew that school hours meant the time that the school bus was running. He admitted his offense, and he knew that the principal had no choice but to fire him as a bus driver. He hated to lose the job. Hated it bad, because he was counting on the money he could save for a ticket and some clothes to take to Rochester with him.

So when school was out, Amos was broke, and would have to hang around for at least a week to help with the tobacco. The crop still had to be treated one more time, and there was a soybean field that needed plowing. If he stayed to help with that for a few days, he thought, either his mother or his granddaddy would let him have enough money to make the trip. He decided not to worry about it. The best thing to do was to handle it just like you'd handle a girl—take it easy. Don't push too fast. Don't get all worked up too soon. Try to stay in control of the situation.

The Falcon was nearing Ernest's house now on the ten-mile drive from Kingstree, and Amos wheeled into the sandy driveway on an impulse. He did not especially want to go home, because he did not want to work this afternoon. Besides, he needed to talk with Ernest about their plans that night. Geraldine was a nice girl, and he liked her and wanted to keep her that way. He already had a date with her Sunday and he knew she would go to the party with him next Tuesday. Tonight he was in the mood for a different kind of girl. He did not have a date. He and Ernest were just going out and pick up something. Sort of a last fling before Ernest left for Florida.

Ernest's mother did not know where her son was. A little while ago, she had noticed him taking a nap out on the back porch. But she had not seen him lately. Amos might try over to the McClary house.

Amos thought a moment and then decided he would go on home. There was still time to get some work done, or at least change the tractor wheels.

"Tell him I'll see him tonight," Amos said to Mrs. Tisdale. As he turned back onto the highway, he thought the nap on the back porch was a good idea. If his back porch had been shaded, he might have done the same thing.

Amos turned off the highway a hundred yards or so beyond Ernest's house and followed the paved secondary road to the right for another mile. He sometimes thought that this stretch of road was the best place to drive in the summertime. The trees were high on either side of the road, and the Spanish moss hanging all over them kept the sun away except in the middle of the day. You could feel the change in air temperature almost as soon as you turned off the main highway. But the mossy trees and the shade were gone when Amos reached the sandy lane turning left into the farm. The corn in the field beside the road was so tall that it almost hid the road and even the big sign advertising Sun Drop Cola on the top and Raymond Scott's Grocery on a strip across the bottom.

Amos turned the car onto the soft sand of the road, and immediately the tires began throwing up a cloud of dust that seemed to hang in the air for a little while before settling back over the Falcon's tracks. When Amos turned into the yard of his grandfather's grocery store a hundred yards down the lane, the dust was still roiling around the car as he opened the door.

The store is a little two-room building that Raymond Scott built himself seventeen years ago. It sits just far enough back from the lane so that two cars can pull into the front yard side by side, allowing the lane to stay free for cars going past the store to the half a dozen houses scattered about in the fields and woods for perhaps a mile beyond. Two cars cannot pass on the lane, and so the store yard is sometimes a handy siding.

The store was built on wooden pillars; the front porch stands about two or three feet off the ground, reachable by a loose stone and one precarious wooden step. The porch is cluttered with assorted wooden soft-drink crates, which are usually upended and serving as seats, and on one side of it is a hand-operated kerosene pump. There is barely room for someone on the porch to operate the electric gas pump, which stands close against the building. The main room of the store is very small and packed with an assortment of canned goods, soft-drink boxes, a cooler for packaged meats, numerous headache remedies and patent medicines, cigarettes and chewing tobacco, and sundry items for home and tool shed.

Even smaller is the back room, where Raymond Scott lives because he cannot abide some of his relatives and because, at the age of seventy, he has achieved a degree of independence that few black men of his station ever know. He is the patriarch, by hard work and inheritance, of a fairly sizable estate. He owns twenty-four acres on the home place, which was left to him by his father. It has been in the family since Raymond Scott's great-grandfather bought it for as little as fifty cents an acre during Reconstruction times. The estate was once 150 acres. But there were many heirs through the years, and some of them were not as good at husbanding the land as Raymond Scott has been, and so most of the original estate was dissipated by bad crop years, bad judgment and shrewd mortgage holders.

In addition to the home place, Raymond Scott also owns a thirty-one-acre farm a few miles away that he inherited from his wife when she died several years ago. He owns the little grocery store, which does not net him a whole lot of money. And he owns the six-room house 200 yards down the lane, which he lets rent-free to his daughter and son-in-law—Amos's parents.

A few years ago, the Scott farms held tobacco allotments totaling slightly more than five acres. But attrition within the government's tobacco-support program has whittled the total allotment down now to just over two acres, and so Raymond Scott must rent additional acreage to make farming worthwhile and justify his investment of around $8,000 in machinery. Altogether, then, Raymond Scott farms about seven and a half acres of tobacco, including his own, a couple that he rents, and two and a half acres that he farms on shares with a widow. If his courtship of the widow is fruitful, he expects someday to add her forty-two-acre farm to his own holdings and move out of his room in the back of the store.

As they affect Amos, finances within the Scott-Jones

families are complicated. Amos's father lives in his father-in-law's house, but he does not farm the Scott land. Ernest Jones and Raymond Scott are cut from distinctly different patterns; Ernest Jones is a sharecropper farming about four acres of tobacco owned by a white man. From time to time, he also takes public work, sometimes in a steel mill at Georgetown and frequently as a migrant following the tobacco harvest. Although Raymond and his son-in-law do not have much to do with one another, Raymond tacitly allows his machinery to be used in making both his own and his son-in-law's crop. Therefore, Amos, his brothers and their mother work for two masters. When Amos cranks up the tractor, he is never really sure whether he will be plowing his father's crop or his grandfather's, unless he is working the corn, soybeans or cucumbers, all of which belong to his grandfather.

That Saturday afternoon after graduation, Amos knew he would be working for his grandfather for at least two days because he had to change the wheels on the tractor. The wheel base of an all-purpose tractor on a small farm must be adjustable so that the tractor can run along one row of tobacco on narrow width or two roys of soybeans on wide width without damaging the young crop. On some models the adjustment is very easy. The front axles are unbolted, slipped out to the required width, and rebolted. The rear wheels have a semiautomatic system that requires only a loosening of the nuts and a spin of the wheel to reposition it. But his grandfather's Ford tractor was, in Amos's considered judgment, a real bastard for wheel changing. The tractor had to be jacked up in the rear, and each of the two rear wheels removed and switched. Each wheel was shaped so that it was either concave or convex, depending on which width was running. Simply by flipping a wheel around, the tire could be placed close against the mud-fender or six inches away from it. But the wheel could not be flipped on the Scott tractor because that would change the direction of the cleats in the tread of the tire. On the Scott tractor the only acceptable method for changing the wheels was to take the right rear wheel and place it on the left axle and put the left wheel on the right axle. Amos had done it hundreds of times in his life, and he liked it less every time he did it.

Meyers and Mickey, Amos's younger brothers, were waiting for him at the store when he drove up. They had not been sure that Amos would get back from town in time to change the tractor, but they knew it was wise to wait for him, just in case. Amos finished washing down a cold soda and then sent his brothers across the road to the tool shed with instructions to bring the tractor and the tools to the store yard. He would be back to start the work as soon as he changed clothes.

Amos drove the Falcon down to the house and parked it on the shady side, next to the water pump on the back porch. Stripping hurriedly to the waist, he worked the lever of the pump until a good stream of water was pouring into the tub beneath the spout. He washed his hands and then ducked his head into the remaining trickle of water. Grabbing a towel from a nail on the wall, he rubbed it through his hair, over his face and across his thin mustache, and tenderly daubed around the large hair bumps on his neck where the beard began. He left the water on his body from the neck to the waist because it would help to cool him as it dried. The house inside was like an oven, and he changed quickly into work clothes, leaving the shirt unbuttoned. On the way out, he completed dressing by taking his blue baseball cap off the dresser and placing it just right on his head so that the visor tipped downward to shield his eyes from the sun.

Amos is built like his father—short and unusually broad-shouldered and thin-waisted, like a welterweight. But he has his mother's face, especially the eyes. Amos's eyes have an Oriental quality about them and, at the same time, a sort of bedroom quality. His eyes seem to be saying always that they see something other eyes do not see, something secret, something private. They are clear, but they are almost hidden by the coal-black skin. Amos is the handsomest of the Fantastic Four, as he has suspected from time to time. He does not have the maturity to match Ernest Tisdale's quiet, easy competence, or the personality of Willie and James. But Amos is also probably the most street-savvy of the group—alert, inquisitive and tough.

By the time Amos got back to the store, Meyers and Mickey had unhooked the disk harrow from behind the tractor and had it in the store yard, ready for jacking up. Instead of doing the work himself, Amos wanted his brothers to do it under his supervision, because he knew they would have to change the wheels without anybody to help them after next week. The job went slowly. It was suppertime before they had the wheels changed, the cultivator hooked up and the tractor gassed and ready for work Monday morning.

Amos's grandfather sat on the porch of the store while the boys worked. He rocked back and forth on an upended bottle crate, shouting occasional directions or harsh warnings first to his three grandsons at the tractor and then to Wayne, the ten-year-old grandson who was tending the counter inside.

It was too bad, Raymond Scott thought, that Amos was so bound and determined to leave the farm. He liked the boy, even though he did look like his daddy. Wasn't like his daddy, though. Amos didn't drink. He was smart, too, and a good worker. A boy like that could make it on the farm nowadays if he really wanted to, especially when he already had the land and the equipment to get a start. Raymond had raised three boys and three girls of his own and half raised Ernest Jones's six boys—and raised the one girl, Marea. She had been like his own daughter, and she wanted to amount to something. He sent her to college and she went to work as a schoolteacher, the same as one of his own daughters had. But all of them had left—all except Amos's mother. Once, she, too, had left. Followed that husband of hers down to Florida back about ten years ago. But they had come back, and he was glad to have them because they were the only family he had living at home now. Yes. Amos would make a good farmer. But he had already seen the city, had money in his pockets, had learned how to get credit. To be a farmer you can't be like some people that look for nothing but sundown and payday, sundown and payday. You got to work and deny and trade. Live right. Live on the land. Pay cash and don't let nobody else do your figuring for you. Raymond knew he was smarter, with his second-grade education, than half the high-school graduates getting out of school nowadays. He had figured close and traded hard. And he had made it. He had been down a few times. One year he was down to nothing but a dead mule and a bony cow. He sold the cow for nineteen dollars, bought two bags of fertilizer and some seed, and started all over again. If he could do it, these boys could do it nowadays. They don't have to work for the white man either. Lot of good colored farmers need sharecroppers and labor. If he was starting all over again, Raymond thought, he would stay right where he was.

Plowing the soybeans Monday, Amos wondered all day if anything was ever going right for him again. The last fling with Ernest Saturday night had been a bust. They hadn't found anything worth messing with. They had gone by Duffy's Garage—to the club in the back half of the garage—and drunk a beer, which Amos did not really want. They had talked a while, made some halfhearted passes at a couple of girls, and then they had just driven around, talking some more. Amos was tired from wrestling with the tractor in the hot sand, and he went home early and watched television for a while before going to bed.

Sunday had not gone too well either. Geraldine was a nice girl, a real sweet girl. He liked her ways an awful lot. But she mixed him up. He wanted her, and yet he did not want to spoil her. He had really known her only a few weeks, and sometimes he thought she was the woman he wanted to marry. He wanted to get involved with her. But he knew he could not allow himself to get involved. Geraldine wanted him to stay in South Carolina, and he did not want to stay—knew he couldn't. He had too many things to do, too many places to go and see. He wanted to make some money, get himself started in a good career. He liked South Carolina. It would be a good place to come back to sometime and raise a family if he could get some money ahead or get a good skill that he could use. Maybe he might come back next year when Geraldine graduated and marry her. He didn't know. He left her early—left vaguely troubled and unsatisfied—and stopped by Ernest's house again. Ernest would be leaving Monday morning for Florida, and Amos knew he would be in the fields all morning.

They worked out a deal. Ernest thought he might not like living with his brother in Florida. If it didn't work out, he would let Amos know and then maybe he would come up to Rochester. Amos knew he could find Ernest a job and a place to live. Maybe they could get an apartment together. There would be more girls in Rochester than Amos could handle, anyway.

It was Tuesday before Amos snapped out of his bad mood. Herman's check for forty dollars came in the mail that day while Amos was suckering tobacco. That was his ticket money and some left over. Then his mother gave him twenty dollars, and Amos knew he would really have something to celebrate at the party Aunt Stella Mae was having for him that night.

Amos took Geraldine to the party, and she cried when he took her home. But this time it did not bother him much.

His father already had left for work at the steel plant when Amos got out of bed Wednesday morning, and so Amos took his time about getting ready. His mother fried an egg and made a boloney sandwich for his breakfast, and when he had eaten, Amos volunteered to drive his mother to the tobacco field half a mile away. Marea, who had come out from town to see him off and to help her mother with the tobacco, told Amos she would pack his bag for him and make some sandwiches to take with him.

When he wanted to kid his mother, or when he felt that his mother needed some kidding, Amos would drop the usual "Mamma" and address her instead as "Sister" or "Miss Jones." In the car going to the tobacco field, Amos sensed that his mother needed some kidding. He tried to think of something to say, and finally decided against kidding her. He told her instead not to worry about him. Yes, he would watch his money and the company he kept. Yes, he would write or call at least once a week. His mother cried only on the inside until she returned home that afternoon to realize that his bag and his clothes were gone.

Marea had packed the bag and was making some sandwiches when Amos got back to the house. He would be on the bus a long time, he told her, so he would need right many. When Marea finally satisfied him she had packed into a paper bag nine boloney sandwiches, a large piece of cake and several cookies.

Elijah Scott and Haywood Tisdale came by for Amos about ten o'clock, and Amos gave Meyers the key to the Falcon with some stern warnings about taking care of it. Marea saw the blue baseball cap a few minutes after they had left in Haywood's car. She looked at it for a moment, and then put it on her head and started walking out to the tobacco field to help her mother.

Elijah was taking a bus North, too, so they went together into the little building on Longstreet Street that the bus station shares with a dress shop and the Williamsburg Chamber of Commerce.

One-way to Rochester, N.Y., was $34.85. Amos put the ticket into his shirt pocket, and he and Elijah and Haywood drove around town for about half an hour killing time until the bus came.

Chapter Twelve
WINDOW SEAT

Old hands among the Seaboard conductors have developed a surprisingly accurate rule of thumb over the years to measure the size of the workload they can expect on any given run with Number 76. "Look at Kingstree," they tell the newer men. "You can tell by Kingstree how many you'll pick up at Dillon and Weldon." Dillon is the last stop in South Carolina; Weldon is the last stop in North Carolina and the last big pickup stop south of Washington.

Conductor W. R. Blackley, who got on at Florence, had had the rule passed on to him years ago, and he remembered it now and passed it on to the man standing with him as the train pulled out of Florence. He could not account for it, Blackley said. "I don't know why it works but it works. Kingstree is the key."

On this particular day, the rule of thumb would be off considerably on Dillon—only twenty-seven would board there—and pretty close on Weldon, where thirty-eight would board. The surprise was Florence, where the Chickenbone Special picked up 196 passengers, four coaches, one dining car and one Pullman. All this was added to the 150 or so passengers and six coaches that the train was pulling when it arrived in Florence, including one hot car that was still not cooling the Kingstree passengers adequately, even after the twenty-minute delay in Florence for repair work.

By the time it rolled into Richmond that night, the train would be carrying about 465 paying passengers plus maybe fifty children riding free and some non-revenue riders, and there would be standing room only.

Donnie and Harim had stayed with the hot car, and now, as the train crossed into North Carolina, Donnie was beginning to feel the effects of the heat and the long ride. He had ventured out of his seat only once, to go to the men's room at the back of the car, and had decided to explore the next car. That had been a mistake, and he did not look forward to it again. The forward motion and sideways lurching of the cars as he walked had triggered the beginning of motion sickness, and he felt dizzy by the time he got back to his seat.

He picked up one of Harim's comic books and spent a few minutes reading about "Binky's Buddies" to get his mind off the dizziness. The four of them—Donnie and Harim and Viola and Rosetta—had talked a lot at first. About Williamsburg County and school and the choir trips to Columbia, about people back home and of course about New York; but not much about New York, for some reason.

Viola had been to the city before, the Bronx, and she and Donnie talked about it for a while.

"What's it like?" Donnie asked. "Is it like the pictures?"

"Well, I don't know. Some things are the same and some are worse and some are better," Viola said.

Donnie told her about some of the things he was looking forward to seeing—Central Park and the Mets, the skyscrapers, the Statue of Liberty, the subway. But Viola could not get excited about it.

"Don't expect too much when you get up there," she said.

"What you mean?"

"Well, just don't expect too much, that's all. Because some things are not like you might think they are. A lot of things you see in the pictures are not there."

They both decided they would adopt the Afro hair style when they got there. Donnie had wanted to go Afro in school, but the principal would not allow any of the kids to do it. Donnie did not understand why. It didn't mean anything. It was just a style, and he liked it. But he had got his hair cut about a week ago, and it was real short, just like it always was. But he did not plan to get another one until it grew out.

The talk sort of drifted into just sitting, listening to Harim's radio and trying to pick up stations, and Donnie kept thinking about New York. "I just hope it's the way I think it is. Not as bad as people say it is," he said to himself again and again.

Donnie had swapped seats with Harim, and he was

Window Seat

sitting in the window seat, on the sunny side, as the train raced north from one little town to another through the eastern North Carolina tobacco fields. Donnie was not at all sure that the view through the window was worth the heat of the late-afternoon sun.

"The land up here looks just like it does at home," he thought. "Except that the tobacco does not look as good." But that was because it was set later. Also, he noticed, there was almost no cotton. The houses along the tracks were all about the same except that in a few towns he saw new brick houses, big ones, that belonged to colored people. He could tell because people were in the yards or on porches, and they waved a lot to the train passengers. The towns looked about the same, but he liked to go through them anyway, looking at the stores and the streets and the people. And the crowds at the train stations.

In one town—he didn't know the name of it—he saw a boy on a bicycle at the station, and he got to thinking about the bicycle he and Jessie had owned one time. All his life he had wanted one, and finally, four or five years ago, Otis had come home one Saturday with a bike in the car. He had bought it in North Carolina secondhand for thirty-five dollars. It really wasn't much good, but Otis told Julia they wanted one so bad that he just got it for them. It lasted about a month, and they must have used up a dozen tubes in that month. He and Jessie didn't know much about fixing tubes, and he guessed the trouble was that they kept pinching them putting new ones in. Sometimes they would put too much air in, or sand would get inside and rub a hole in the tube. They couldn't go on putting tubes in, so they had put it in the barn. About a year ago, Julia had thrown it out in the garbage, and that was that. It was an English racer.

That seemed like a long time ago. He was not interested in bikes any more. What he wanted now was a car, a Firebird or a Stingray. He had been saying for a long time that there were only three things he was interested in when he got out of school—a good house, a good car, and a good wife, one that would stick with a man and not expect too much out of him. He had not met that kind of girl yet, maybe because he had not dated much in high school. Jessie had to take the car to work, so there was no way to date much. But he wasn't that interested anyway. It could lead to trouble. It almost had with him. "I wonder what's going to happen to her," he thought.

That had been back in the spring, and they had sex together. She was that kind of girl. Everybody had with her, and that's what he had gone for. But he didn't count on what happened. He heard later she was pregnant; he lived in agony for a couple of weeks, at least. Turned out a lot of others were scared, too. But it wasn't his. He knew it and she knew it, and so nothing came of it as far as he was concerned. But he still wondered what would happen to her. He wondered about New York, and what kind of girls he would meet there. Living with a sister might get pretty dull in New York, he guessed.

New York. He thought he might apply first for a job in the post office. That is what Belle told him to do. But he was not sure that was what he wanted. One time he had thought about being a mechanic. But he gave that up because it dirtied up too many clothes. He thought he might like to go to a trade school to learn about electronics. He liked to mess around with radios and phonos. He was not sure he wanted a job that meant standing up or walking all the time. Since he got his leg hurt playing baseball his sophomore year, he couldn't do much of that. The leg was still buckling on him every once in a while. That was one reason he wasn't much of a dancer.

Of course, if he couldn't find a job, he figured he might just come on back down South. Otis and Julia wanted him to come back. They hadn't wanted him to leave. They did not understand it, and he was not sure he could understand it himself. New York was New York. It was all those pictures Belle kept sending back, maybe. Whatever it was, he was on his way. "I'm gonna see it for myself," he thought. "I've got to see it for myself."

Donnie was half asleep when he noticed that the countryside through the window had become blurred. The train had run into a heavy rainstorm just south of Rocky Mount. It was almost dark outside, and Donnie at first thought he must have been asleep for a long time. But he looked at his watch and noticed that it was not yet seven o'clock. The darkness was from the clouds and the sheets of rain slapping against the window without making any noise above the noise of the train.

He jerked himself awake, knowing that if he slept now he would not be able to sleep later. But he was tired and his neck ached, and he felt hot and sticky. He decided to do something that was for him, under the circumstances, a very brave thing. He would change clothes right here on the train.

In one of the bags in the rack above was a pair of bell-bottom blue jeans that Renea had sent him from New York a couple of months earlier. He got up and stretched and rubbed his neck, and then reached into the rack and dug out first the jeans, then a blue Paisley sport shirt and finally a pair of tennis shoes.

Gripping all these under one arm and using the other arm to steady himself from seat to seat, Donnie went back to the men's room at the end of the car. He washed his hands and his face in one of those crazy little sinks where you have to hold the spigot to keep the water running, changed his clothes and came out feeling a whole lot better.

When he had repacked his dress pants and the yellow shirt and the dress shoes, he got the food out of the bag and sat down to eat a sandwich and a piece of fried chicken with Harim and the girls.

Donnie Gibson's fellow passengers on the Chickenbone Special were the same kinds of people—often the same people—who had been riding the train for years.

Willie Snow was one of the lucky ones, an exception really. He had received his degree two weeks earlier at South Carolina State College, got a job with International Paper Company in his hometown of Georgetown, and now was on his way to Jamaica, N.Y., for a vacation, and then fourteen weeks at a company sales-training course in New York City.

Mrs. Annie Montgomery left Kingstree for Nyack,

N.Y., fifteen years ago, and has ridden the train back and forth so many times she can't count them.

Mrs. Mary Whack moved to Philadelphia when she was thirteen years old, and married there. But she still visits her home in Greeleyville at least once a year.

Lewis Keels, a rising senior at Tomlinson High School in Kingstree, was making his second trip to North Philadelphia for summer work at a plastic-bag factory. He would live with his grandmother there until the fall. He would rather stay in Kingstree after graduation. But he assumes that next summer he will move to North Philadelphia permanently.

Mrs. Reeaurther Wilson grew up in Olanta, S.C. She went to Philadelphia in the late forties, married a paper hanger and returned to Florence, S.C., when they learned they could make more money hanging paper there than they could in Philadelphia. But her husband died several years later, and she moved to Paterson, N.J., then back to Olanta from 1957 until 1961, then to a little community on Long Island for six years and finally to Huntington, N.Y., two years ago. She commutes now to a job in Paterson and visits Olanta every chance she gets. Mrs. Wilson has one brother and one sister living in Kingstree, two sisters in Florida, four sisters in Paterson, one brother in Raleigh, N.C., and one brother in Smithfield, N.C.

Ophelia Alford finished high school in Marlboro County, S.C., two years ago, waited a year for a job that never developed in a local textile mill, and then migrated to Newark with a cousin who came down to visit the summer after Ophelia graduated. Six weeks after she got to Newark, she got a job in a city park and saved enough money to enter a school of beauty culture, from which she expected to graduate soon after her return to Newark from this trip.

Ophelia had been back to Marlboro County for her younger sister's high-school graduation. The sister was planning to go to Newark in the fall, after Ophelia sent some information back to her about an IBM school in Newark.

Ophelia's parents died before she was twelve years old, and she had grown up in her grandmother's home, a modest four-room farmhouse with outdoor plumbing. To her the house is "just a regular country house," and she loves it. Even visiting for a week, she finds it difficult to leave the regular country house, with its warmth and its familiarity.

When she thinks about what she wants most in life, the answer comes easy: a house of her own—land of her own, and the opportunity to work profitably as a beautician in her home county.

Patricia Burgess had received her high-school diploma at Lake City the day before she boarded the train. She was on her way to Newark to look for some kind of office work and live with her mother. Patricia had lived with her grandmother in Lake City since the age of one, and, until the summer after her junior year, she had vaguely planned to stay there after high school. By August that year she had become familiar with the labor market and had made her decision to go North after graduation. With her high-school courses in typing, shorthand and general office procedure, she did not expect to have any trouble finding a job in Newark.

Patricia was sharing a seat on the train with her classmate Gloria Cooper. Gloria, the oldest of four children, grew up with her mother. Her father works in a tobacco factory in Maryland. The summers after her sophomore and junior years, Gloria had lived with her aunt in Jamaica, N.Y., working as a clerk-typist in a loan office. She was headed back to Jamaica now to take a permanent job.

James L. Sellers, a rising junior at South Carolina State College, was going to Mount Holly, N.J., where he will live with his mother and find a summer job. When he finishes college in 1971, he will leave the South permanently, as have most of the members of his high-school class of two years ago.

In two years of college weekend visits back to his home in Latta, S.C., Sellers has compiled what he thinks is a fairly accurate record of how many of his high-school classmates have migrated. There were sixty-seven graduates that year, all of them black. Of the sixty-seven, only four live in the county now, to the best of his knowledge, and he has tried to find them. The four are girls, and Sellers believes that they remained in the county only because they are married.

In a sense, James Sellers is representative of a minority within a minority, in that his reasons for leaving the South are social rather than economic. He is fed up with racism and repression and intimidation. He is angry because he cannot go places and do things as a black, and he is disgusted because almost no one, in his opinion, white or black, can go any place or do anything after eleven o'clock at night. He believes that a great many blacks in the South are scared of the Ku Klux Klan. But this opinion has been contradicted repeatedly in both word and action throughout the region. In the South today the black has come to much the same realization as reputable and responsible whites have regarding the Klan—that it is made up of demented, tortured souls, as much to be pitied as feared; ignored, stamped out, but never feared. Whatever can be said of his brothers in the Deep South, the black in the mid-South and upper South is far more concerned with legal harassment and denial by established authority than he is with the illegal intimidation, reprisal and cow-pasture bombast of Klansmen.

If there is a representative black Southerner, it is more likely to be Ophelia Alford than James Sellers.

Ophelia is aware that she is a black in a white society. She is aware that she grew up in social and economic conditions that are less than reasonable in the United States, albeit the Southern part of the United States. To the best of her ability, she will change what can be changed and accept what cannot be changed. If she could get a job as a beautician in the South, would she come back?

Making good money, yes.

What kind of money?

Well. Enough money, like, you know, enough money to put aside for things that I've always wanted for so long. Like a house of my own, land of my own. Something like that. Something I've always wanted.

Why would she come back to the South?

I like the South.

Why?

I was born and raised here. I really like the South.

Despite all the Kluxers?

Yes.

And sometimes the hatred?

Yes.

And the racism?

Yes. It really doesn't bother me. I'd still like to come back here. I mean, I was born and raised here. It's like I just can't get out of place here. Like they say, there's no place like home, and coming back here—just for the week—I hated to even leave. I always hate to leave when I go home.

This love of home, of place, is every bit as strong among whites and blacks as it has been portrayed in song and drama, and strong enough at times to border on chauvinism.

The Southern black is a black first. That is undeniable and unalterable. But he also is a Southerner. That, too, is undeniable and, in a great many instances, unalterable. Socially and culturally, the Southern black is almost a shadow of the Southern white, except where economic conditions are so terrible that they warp the social and cultural structures into grotesque anomalies. Religiously, he is perhaps twenty to forty years behind the white Anglo-Saxon Protestant in the degree of fundamentalism retained. But then he is often considerably ahead of some present-day sects in the region. It is in his love of land, of place, that the Southern black most readily shows his Southernness.

Among native whites it is understandable, because the white Southerner has a deep involvement with history, with place and space and time, that makes him more like himself than any other American.

But how can this Southern sense of belonging held by

native blacks be accounted for? Perhaps it is that, as several have suggested, some of the toughest times of one's life—and the places where one has suffered these times—are rich because one survived and came through. One can look back later and say, "That is the place where I fought it out." And the fact that the Negro has suffered in the South and survived in the South may make the South an even richer land to him than it is to the white man, because he has suffered more in the South than the white man has suffered. Whatever the reason, the attachment exists widely and deeply, and it is far more than simple nostalgia.

Somewhere north of Petersburg, Virginia, just about the time the passengers are becoming bone-weary and approaching a farmer's bedtime, the clickety-click sound underneath the coaches of the Chickenbone Special changes noticeably to a jolting, jostling clickety-clack, interrupted in something like three-quarter time by off-key thuds and thumps. That is the worst time for the passengers in crowded coaches. Later, when the train pulls out of Washington about 2:35 in the morning for its final leg of the trip, fatigue has set in so thoroughly that the body is forced into sleep, despite the pinched leg room and the enforced upright position.

But from Petersburg to Washington, life on the train is about four hours of excruciating and unrelieved tedium as the passengers twist and squirm, riding alternately in a loose sprawl and bolt straight, to put the burden of pain on first one and then another part of the anatomy. The scenery through the window is gone. The water trickling out of the fountains has become tepid—if, indeed, there is any water at all. Conversation has been exhausted. The novelty of the thing, even for first-time passengers, has long since worn out.

In Donnie Gibson's car, there was some periodic relief from the tedium. It came in the person of an aged and toothless laborer to whom Saturday night was Saturday night, whether it was passed on board a train or in a juke joint. "Toothless One" had boarded around sunset somewhere in southside Virginia. He was going to Philadelphia, and he obviously had fortified himself heavily for the journey.

Soon after he boarded, the man decided in his bleary head that he had lost a hat on the train. Later he thought it must have been a coat that he lost. So for about three hours he stalked back and forth through the cars, mumbling, swaying, sometimes nearly falling as he reached up to the baggage racks to inspect various hats and coats.

In Donnie's car, one of the baggage areas he poked into was that of Mrs. Reeaurther Wilson, who had not been a paper hanger for nothing.

"What you doing?" Mrs. Wilson demanded of him.

"Who asked you?" he replied, after staring at her a moment to get her into proper focus. Sizing up the situation, he thought better of his answer and informed Mrs. Wilson and the car in general that somebody had stolen his hat.

"Get out of here, man," Mrs. Wilson told him. "You weren't even in this car in the first place, and you been poking around in this car all night."

"Who asked you?" the man said again. But when

Mrs. Wilson began rising from her seat, he swayed on toward the rear of the car.

At the door he turned to recapture some of his lost dignity. "You people better be careful," he shouted. "I'm a member of the FBI."

This announcement was greeted by raucous laughter, and the Toothless One thereafter became the "Phantom Cop." Later he told a man in another car that he was a highway patrolman, without designating any particular state where he did his patrolling.

The charade ended forcefully and rather sadly in one of the men's rooms, where the Phantom Cop was admiring his blue checked hat, which he had just found in one of the cars. Unfortunately, the hat also had another owner, who had followed the Cop into the men's room. While the owner's left hand held a fist full of shirt and rested against the Phantom Cop's Adam's apple, his right hand jerked the hat from PC's head, jammed it down on his own head and returned to a threatening position immediately in front of and slightly to the right of the Phantom Cop's nose.

"Old man," the owner said, "if you wasn't so old I'd cold-cock you right here. You ain't lost no coat and you ain't lost no hat. Now you find yourself a seat and sit." After that the train was quiet, seemingly filled with even more tedium than before.

Donnie forced himself to stay awake until Washington. He did not know exactly why. Washington was the capital of the United States. He was not sure it was more important than New York, but somehow he felt that visiting Washington for the first time—even passing through it in the middle of the night—was an important event in a person's life. A person ought to be awake for it even if there is nothing more to see than some buildings and monuments with lights shining on them. At the station, he wanted to get out and walk along the platform as some of the others were doing. But he went to the door of the car and knew that he should not chance it. He was not sure how long the train would stay there, and he did not want to get left behind. He went back into the car and bought a soda from the vendor who came through the train. When the soda was gone and the train was not yet in Baltimore, Donnie allowed himself to sleep. His sleep was fitful but it lasted until Trenton became visible in the early-morning light. He realized then that he had not been worried about New York when he fell asleep. There had been no need for a prayer.

Chapter Thirteen
NEW YORK IS ALL RIGHT

The southern approach to New York City is not scenic when it is framed by the window of a train on a hazy morning.

Flying into the city, a passenger can have a breathtaking view across the Hudson River on a good day or night, even through a small window looking across the edge of a wing. And even seen from a car or bus, the silhouette of the Manhattan skyline is enough to quicken the pulse.

But the train goes by way of the industrial back yard of New Jersey, and before the passenger gets much of a look at anything more than factories, scrap yards and salt flats, he is dipped into the darkness below the Hudson to emerge into natural daylight again only by riding up the escalator at Penn Station.

Donnie Gibson did not see New York City at all. He was sitting on the wrong side of the train for proper tourism. The haze shrouded the distant scene, and his eyes burned anyway from a night of restless sleep and many hours of staring out the window. For the first night of his life, Donnie had not slept on a bed, and even his youth and strength could not easily shake off the cumulative ache of eighteen hours on the train. Still, he noticed a peculiar feeling inside himself when the conductor opened the door next to Donnie's seat and announced that New York was the next stop. Donnie's chest tightened and then he knew that his stomach felt funny, as if he needed to go to the bathroom. He could not see New York. But he was almost there. It was like being in Washington, D.C., even when he could not see that he was in Washington, D.C. Only it was worse. Without knowing it, Donnie was afflicted to some extent by what might be called the "Manhattan syndrome"—that is, a feeling that New York City really is the center of the world, that the Hudson River really is civilization's outer limit, separating life from mere existence. Like millions of other hinterland youngsters, Donnie had been subjected since early childhood to a romanticized and largely fictitious image of the nation's largest city. This image had been laid before him constantly, sometimes so subtly as to be subliminal, by television, books, magazines, and the occasional movie that he saw. In Donnie's case, the image had been reinforced by snapshots sent home by his sisters and by personal accounts brought home by brothers and sisters who knew but could not admit to their family at home that their stories of life in the city were not altogether truthful.

Now, Donnie was about to see for himself the place he had heard so much about. In a few minutes his journey would be ended, and he knew that part of the feeling inside him was fear.

By their own trial and error and then by following the crowd, Donnie and Harim found just the right escalator up from the track level. But Belle and Geraldine were waiting for him at the top instead of Renea. Renea was expecting another baby soon and she had not felt up to the trip. They hugged him, and then there was some talk back and forth about how good everybody looked and how things were at home and with the brothers and sisters in Brooklyn, and then Donnie turned to Harim, who was standing back a few feet.

Harim was going to call his brother, but he thought he might mess around the station for a while first, and maybe go up and look around the streets. They grinned at one another and then began laughing. It was Harim who spoke first.

"See ya, man," he said.

"See ya," Donnie said.

Belle picked up one of his bags and the three of them

started up again to the next level, only to cross a little foyer and start down again to the subway level.

"Up and down. Up and down. Is that all New York is?" Donnie asked, taking the steps two and three at a time.

"You better get used to this," Belle said. "You gonna have to ride the subway everywhere in this city."

They passed through the turnstile and then had to wait a few minutes on the subway platform. Donnie saw a penny scale and decided to weigh himself.

"Hundred and fifty," he said. "That's wrong. I weighed one fifty-nine back home."

He bought a Coke from the machine next to the scale and then lit a cigarette. Belle gently took it out of his hand and stepped on it. "The first thing you gotta learn about the subways," she told him, "is that you don't smoke in them. They put you under the jail for that."

The ride to Brooklyn on the Eighth Avenue Subway was noisy to Donnie, and he had trouble talking with Geraldine, sitting next to him. So mostly he just sat with a silent laugh on his face, watching the station platforms pass by. He wondered if the Mets would be playing in New York today and if he would have time to go to see them.

The train had pulled into New York a little after 7:00, and it was not yet 9:00 when Donnie and his sisters emerged into the sunlight again at the Clinton and Washington Avenue stop. It was a beautiful morning, sunny and still cool. The streets were quiet and almost deserted. Donnie noticed that there were no skyscrapers. Just big old brick buildings that looked pretty nice to him. He noticed the garbage also.

New York Is All Right

"Don't you have garbage pickup in Brooklyn?" he asked Geraldine.

"What you mean?" she said. "Sure we have garbage pickup. They just picked it up this morning."

Donnie pointed to the cans sitting along the sidewalk with the loose garbage lying around them. "They don't do such a good job," he said.

At the corner of Washington and Gates Avenue, they stopped and Geraldine pointed to the right, down Gates. "See the building down the street there?" she asked, giving some closer instructions. "That's where Belle and I live." She and Belle are not married, and they share an apartment. But Donnie could not figure out which building they were talking about because they all looked like one building to him. His sisters settled instead for showing him the little grocery store on Washington where they did most of their shopping.

Renea's apartment was half a block up Gates, to the left of Washington, and Donnie recognized Kevin's maroon Buick parked in front. Kevin and Renea had driven South in it last Easter when they brought little Glenn down to stay with Julia until after the new baby came.

Renea and her husband, Kevin, pay $112 a month for a $3\frac{1}{2}$-room basement apartment in one of the Brooklyn brownstones. The rent supposedly includes furniture, but the Poches added some of their own to make it attractive and livable. They have not been able to control the roach problem.

The living room has a window facing onto the street that begins below sidewalk level and rises slightly above it. Behind the living room, in a straight line running to the back of the house, there is a half-room separated from the living room by an archway decorated by the Poches with ornamental chains hanging from the top of the arch, Oriental fashion. The chains are made in a metal shop where Donnie's brother Leon works. Behind the half-room is the bedroom, and behind the bedroom is the kitchen with a bar for dining. To the left behind the bar, there is a closet and a bathroom, which Renea has improved considerably with paint and pretty linens. There is another window and a door leading out of the kitchen into a small back yard. It is the type of apartment that would be called "shotgun" in the South because of its barrel-straight arrangement of rooms.

The living room also shows the results of Renea's homemaking talent. It is small, like the other rooms, but it is comfortable and homey. The sofa has a matching sectional piece for the opposite corner. The coffee table has two matching end tables at either side of the sofa. The showpiece of the room is Kevin's stereo, long and low, with a built-in bar that swivels around to serving position to show a bright-red felt lining.

Everything works in the apartment except the doorbell, which has been replaced by a recognition system within the family—Renea's brothers and sisters and Kevin's brother Stan. They announce themselves by rapping on the living-room window as Belle did the Sunday morning of Donnie's arrival.

Kevin answered the door. Renea was back in the kitchen making breakfast. Belle had called her from Penn Station, and the smell of sausage frying now filled the apartment. Kevin led them through the door, past another door, or gate of iron bars, into a hallway and then into the living room, where Donnie was assaulted in a flying leap by Sheila, Geraldine's four-year-old daughter. Normally, Sheila lives in South Carolina with her grandmother. She and one of Belle's two girls, Jackie, were visiting their mothers for part of the summer.

"Hi, Sheila. How's my girl?" Donnie said, as he grabbed her and twirled her around the room. He then got the same welcome from Jackie, who had been slower leaving the television set in the bedroom, and the three of them wallowed on the sofa until Renea called Donnie for breakfast.

Over breakfast of eggs, sausage and pancakes, Kevin told Donnie about his own work and what Donnie might expect in New York. Kevin had come North from New Orleans four years ago and got a make-do job plastering until he could find something better. His philosophy is that work of any sort is no good. "But you gotta get things the best way you can," he told Donnie, "and that means by working. So you work. Instead of coming home at the end of forty hours feeling good but with no money in my pocket, I'd rather work eighty hours and come home tired but knowing that I've earned something."

It is that kind of philosophy that has sustained Kevin through the schedule he maintains. He leaves home five days a week at 2:30 in the afternoon to drive to his second-shift job as a foreman in a tire-retreading shop in New Jersey. When he completes the eight-hour shift there, he drives to a plastics factory nearby, where he puts in another eight hours for six days each week. When he has completed the forty-mile round trip, he gets to sleep about 9:30 or 10:00 each morning.

Kevin's eleven-day eighty-eight-hour week returns him $310 a week, part of which goes into a savings account. With a third baby coming, he knew that he would have to move his family soon. He would like very much to buy a house somewhere on Long Island, and if he could hold out for a year, if he had any luck at all, he thought they could do it.

He told Donnie that he thought there might be an opening coming up at the retread shop. They could look into it later. In the meantime something better might come up. Donnie did not expect any trouble finding some sort of job, maybe a pretty good one. Archie was doing pretty good. He was a supervisor at an industrial home for the blind. Leon was in good shape. But they had had a baby not long ago, and they were going to have to move out of the two-room apartment. Belle still thought the Post Office Department, where she worked, was a good bet, but Geraldine would check around at the discount store where she had a job.

After breakfast, Donnie called South Carolina to tell Otis and Julia he had arrived without getting into any trouble.

"Julia?" he said. "I made it. Yes'm. No trouble at all. Just sore from riding. How's Otis? Well, tell him I made it. Yes'm, they're right here."

As the others took turns talking to their parents, Donnie took Sheila's hand and went out into the hallway.

"I'm taking Sheila for a walk up the street," he told

Geraldine. He figured he could find the little store his sisters had pointed out and maybe even their apartment building.

He was back an hour later, carrying a large box of cornflakes and a quart of milk.

"Boy, this is some big place," he said, opening the cornflakes and heading toward the kitchen.

He poured a glass of milk and drank it in the kitchen. Then he poured out a bowl of cereal, splashed some milk over it, and retired to the bedroom, where he ate and watched television from the bed while his sisters started Sunday dinner. They had called Archie and Leon, and both of them were coming over later with their wives.

Donnie watched part of one program and then another one all the way through before he became restless again. This time he announced that he was taking Jackie for a walk. He still had $4.48 left after buying the cornflakes and milk. He thought he might find another store open.

It was on his second walk through the streets of Brooklyn that first Sunday in New York that Donnie knew everything was going to be all right. Kids were playing along the sidewalks now. He could hear music coming from some of the open windows, and he noticed for the first time that there were trees along the streets.

"New York is all right," he thought. "I think I'm gonna like it. It's gonna be like I thought it was."

Kevin was shaving and Renea was cutting and rolling out noodles when Donnie had slammed the outside door on his way out of the apartment.

"That boy!" Renea said. She and Kevin figured they would let him loaf for a week, seeing the city, before they helped him find a job.

Chapter Fourteen
GOOD-BY, MAYFLOWER

The United States Congress and the Bureau of Public Roads have made it relatively painless for the latter-day migrants out of the Southeast to change their place and their way of life. If a man has a car or access to one, and if he has the determination or the desperation to use it, all he needs beyond that is the price of a tank of gas and the ninety-five cents he must render in tribute to the Commonwealth of Virginia for the privilege of traveling over 34.7 miles of highway called the Richmond-Petersburg Turnpike. There is little choice but to pay the money because the turnpike lies like a purse string across the two major north-south highways in the Southeast—Interstate 85 and Interstate 95. The string is drawn tight at Petersburg, where the two highways converge. But south of the turnpike, the roads are free and relatively fast. To get from Warren County, North Carolina, to Washington, D.C., for example, you take 58 and then 158 east to Roanoke Rapids and turn left. Something like three hours later, barring mishap, you will have reached the heart of the city's northwest ghetto without moving the steering wheel more than an inch or so in either direction.

The Alston family caravan had to make one stop the day that Wash and Creola moved their family to Washington. Ernest Turner was out of high-test gas that Saturday morning, and Willie Durham refused to burn anything but high test even when he was driving somebody else's car. So the caravan, Willie in the lead, stopped in Roanoke Rapids to gas up, and it was only then that Creola remembered that she had not had breakfast. Maybe by black man's custom, or maybe because he is Willie Durham, Willie chose a combination gas station and grocery store that looked as if a man could feel at home there and get decent service. While the cars were being filled up by the elderly white man who owned the place, Creola and the older girls went into the dimly lit grocery store to buy a round of soda, milk and cookies for everyone from the owner's wife. The milk tasted good to Creola, but she was not as hungry as she had thought. When they were on the road again, she broke the ten-cent cookie into little pieces and fed it to Hosea on her lap.

The trip had not started well. Wash had not been able to find a truck, and he would have postponed the move except that Willie Durham volunteered to take Wash down to North Carolina in his station wagon for just the gas money. Willie was anxious for Wash to get his family moved in as soon as he could. After all, Willie's house was standing partly empty, and he wanted to get a suitable renter in as quickly as possible. Wash had owned neither a car nor a driver's license in twenty years, and he knew he was dependent on Willie for the move. Thursday, the transmission had gone bad in Willie's station wagon and Wash thought again about canceling the trip. But Willie prevailed. The man at the garage loaned Willie a '62 Dodge compact and assured him it would make the trip even though it had a couple of slick tires.

Wash knew he could not fit the whole family into the little Dodge, so he called Harvey, his oldest boy, and asked him to go down and help bring the family to Washington. Harvey and Gary, the second boy, were living with their aunt in Washington, and Harvey had saved enough money to buy a new Plymouth. But he had not yet learned to drive it, so they called Creola's brother Wiley, who is almost a son because Wash and Creola raised him, and Wiley agreed to go along as the driver.

After Wash got off work Friday evening, he and Willie left Washington. They got into Mayflower about 1:30 in the morning. Willie dropped Wash at the house and then drove on to visit his brother in Franklin County. He agreed to come back early Saturday morning, when the boys would be down from Washington in the second car.

Creola worried about the moving arrangements. She especially did not like the thought of leaving Hosea's crib behind. That meant that Hosea would have to sleep with her and Wash until they could go back South for the furniture. But she was glad to have Wash home, to have the family together again, and she trusted the Lord that He would help them move the furniture soon enough. Wash had met this man in Washington who drove a dump truck. He thought he might be able to get it, or maybe a pickup, and come back next week for the furniture. Creola was sorry also that she would not be able to leave as early Saturday as Wash wanted to. She had hung out her last washing Friday afternoon, and a sudden thunderstorm had struck the neighborhood. The clothesline broke, dumping most of the clothes into the rain and mud before she could get them inside. She salvaged some of the baby's things and hung them over the chair next to the wood stove in the living room. But everything else had to be taken in to the self-service laundry in Warrenton Saturday morning.

Wiley and his wife, Alta, took Creola into Warrenton to do the washing and dropped Wash off at Ernest Turner's store. Wash had to make the arrangements about the house and the land. He was the last of the Alstons to leave the South—seven brothers and four sisters had preceded him to the North—and he had decided to ask Ernest to look out for the place. He wanted to pay some on the grocery bill, too, but Ernest told him not to worry about it.

"You gonna need your money for a while," Ernest said. "You get your family settled in Washington, and then we can settle up later."

Although he is still in his early forties, Ernest Turner has become the patriarch of the Mayflower community. There are a few men older than Ernest, but he is the man who has fought longest and most successfully for the civil rights, the economic welfare and the human dignity of the blacks. He is a roly-poly man of immense energy and with a streak of waggish mischief about as wide as his waistline. Now and then, just for the hell of it, he will precede a comment on whatever happens to be under discussion at the moment with, "Well, when I used to be a nigger. . . ." Despite his own laughter, he means it when he says frequently that he has not been a nigger since 1954.

Ernest took over the little family farm and the store when he returned from the Navy in World War II. Neither the farm nor the store—both of them together, for that matter—was profitable enough to support his family and his parents. Ernest went into public work and used his salary to build up the farm. He taught returning veterans in an agriculture program for a while, and then worked in the post office until the local white power structure decided he was too uppity. With luck, some sharp dealing and a lot of hard work, he has achieved a modest degree of success. He is up at 5:30 every morning and usually eats his supper around 11:00 every night, while watching the late news. His workday is spent attending to first one business and then another —the one-room store half a mile from his house, a dry-cleaning plant in Warrenton, his cucumber buying shed if it is the cucumber season, or the tobacco fields if it is tobacco season. Ernest's allotment is small, and his land is tired and not very productive. But he has two good tractors and the cash and credit to provide seed and fertilizer, so he and two or three other men in the community usually can piece together a communal allotment of around seven acres of tobacco.

Ernest would be a rich man except that he has been president of the Warren County NAACP chapter for the past ten years. That cut off his credit in town for a while, and it has cut heavily into his hustling time for personal security. Somehow, he finds time to haul neighborhood children to the Head Start program, canvass the county to pack the Social Security rolls with every eligible black he can find, and march in the streets of Warrenton when it is necessary to knock down one or another racial barrier in a town that once was a prime example of Old South white supremacy. He still refers to himself and other blacks as "colored people."

Wash Alston knew his property would be in good hands with Ernest. Ernest agreed to pay Wash $250 a year rent on the land. He would try also to find somebody to live in the house. He thought he could get maybe fifteen dollars a month for it. But Wash knew he could not count on that. There were not many potential renters left in the county. Normally, Ernest would have sent the rent money to Wash after crops were harvested in the fall, but he knew Wash needed it in advance.

It was close to 10:30 when the family started packing up the two cars, and only then did they discover that the trunk on Willie Durham's borrowed Dodge would not open. That meant that there would be no jack in case of a flat, and also that Creola and the kids had to start weeding out much of the clothing and personal belongings they had intended to take.

In the end, they packed little more than some dishes and a change of clothing for everyone. Creola remembered to pack her special medicated shampoo. But she forgot her hymnbook, a lapse that cost her a great deal of secret worry and prayer in the next several days.

Soon after 11:00, the cars were packed and everybody was assigned a seat or partial seat. Creola pulled the front door closed and latched it against the wind, for it never had held a lock. She did not look back when the cars turned out of the front yard and up the lane. The Dodge scraped as it bounced through the biggest mudhole—the one by the paved road. Willie Durham could not judge its depth because water filled it for a car length. Also, Willie was in a hurry by this time. He went on toward Ernest Turner's store, but Creola had to stop first at Susie Alston's house. Susie was a dear friend and a distant relative. In Mayflower, half the families are Alstons, just as Creola was before she married an Alston.

The shoeman would be by next Wednesday to collect the last payment on the boys' shoes, and Creola left the $1.50 with Susie.

"Pray for me," she called to Susie as she got back in the car.

"Bless you. I will," Susie said. "We all will be praying for you. Take care, now, and let us hear from you."

Susie had been North once years ago, and she had got so sick of it that she didn't know what to do except come back to her Warren County house, which feels as if it is going to fall apart every time the wind blows strong.

The Alstons said good-by to Ernest and Dottie Turner quickly because Willie Durham was in a hurry to find some high-test gas. The cars were carrying fifteen people—Wash and Creola and ten of their eleven children, plus Wiley, his wife, Alta, and Willie Durham. Willie hardly slowed down when he turned off the paved secondary road onto Highway 58 near the church. Creola knew she must send up one of her little prayers.

"Dear Lord," she said, looking straight ahead and seeing only her God, "Dear Lord, give us a safe trip. Guide the steering wheels of these cars that we might have a safe trip. Ride the highways with us and go with us into our new house in Washington."

They turned onto the broad concrete of Interstate 95 soon after the gas stop in Roanoke Rapids, and Willie, carrying most of the older children in his car, quickly left the second car behind.

Creola had made a pot of stew, some potato salad and a coconut cake Friday, and she packed it in the trunk of the Plymouth Saturday morning with the dishes. She thought it might be pleasant to stop somewhere alongside the road for a picnic. But the Interstate is not an especially inviting place for black people off the farm to stop for picnics, and she could not stop unless the whole family stopped. Willie Durham was far ahead of them throughout the trip, and Creola kept looking for them along the road, hoping to see them waiting for the Plymouth to catch up, yet hoping not to see them because it might mean car trouble. Just beyond Richmond they ran into a severe rainstorm, and Creola forgot her hopes for a picnic. Anyway, it would be good to have the food all ready when they got to Washington. Everybody would be hungry then, and she would not have to worry about cooking on a strange stove.

Creola was content during most of the trip except for the little worry in the back of her mind about Willie's car and the chance of an accident. She thought cars traveled awfully fast on the superhighways. She sat quietly rocking little Hosea on her lap by bouncing her knees or swaying them back and forth in the little bit of leg room she had. Hosea responded by sleeping through most of the trip. When he waked now and then, Creola would pass him to Wash or Bernice, the thirteen-year-old, to give her legs a rest. When Hosea got fretful, Creola would take him back and quiet him again.

Creola wondered about the house, but she did not really worry about it. Wash had answered most of her questions, and she trusted his judgment. It was heated, and it had a yard in the back for the kids to play in. That was all that really mattered, she reckoned. Secretly, she sort of looked forward to living in Washington for a personal reason. With a salary coming in regular now, she might be able to get her teeth fixed. She wanted some new teeth in front awfully bad.

More than anything else, Creola thought about the church and worried about whether she would find one that she liked, that she could feel at home in. She remembered Ernest Turner's remark that last preaching Sunday. Ernest had laughed when he told her, "Now don't you go up there and turn Holiness."

Creola knew that Ernest was serious when he said that, despite his laughter. She understood his concern and shared it. Creola was saved to Christ the summer when she was fourteen. She and her sister Rosetta went to a revival service at Spring Green Church up in the northern part of the county because they knew the time had come to accept Jesus as their personal Savior. They went to the revival to be saved, and they did not wait for the preacher to make his altar call. The spirit moved the girls while the preacher was still preaching; they got up together, tears streaming down their cheeks, and marched down the aisle to kneel at the mourners' bench. On a warm Sunday morning the following September, the girls were baptized in Shocco Creek by the old pastor then serving at Saint Stephen. That was in 1942, and Creola had been a faithful and devoted member of Saint Stephen's ever since. She had taught herself to read and then studied and educated herself at night while her children studied, partly because she wanted to be able to read and understand and interpret the Bible. She had grown up in her church, and she had changed over the years as her church had changed.

Creola's religion in the summer of 1969 was not the same religion that her grandfather had practiced as a jackleg preacher forty years earlier. Her church was not the kind of church her grandfather would have felt at home in. It was not, in fact, exactly the kind of church it had been when the old pastor had baptized Creola in 1942. Saint Stephen had matured, had grown away from the raw emotion of old-time worship. If one of the older sisters of the church feels the need now and then to shout when the spirit moves her, that is all right. The other members of the congregation appreciate her feeling and enjoy it with her. But the service at Saint Stephen usually is conducted with dignity and a stately grace that is lacking in some of the more primitive congregations. This is at once a matter of immense pride and a source of concern among members of the congregation, for there are some families in the surrounding countryside—even in the Mayflower community itself—who do not appreciate the staid kind of religion practiced at Saint Stephen. A few, a very few nowadays, still take their religious guidance from the same source that ministers to their medical and emotional problems—the root doctor who lives a mile or so down the road from the Alston place. The church members tolerate the competition from the root doctor because his practice is not a real threat to the church. In fact, a few of the more superstitious church members have been known to call on the root doctor in times of severe crisis. This is not seen as a matter of backsliding exactly, because the supplicant almost always puts his first faith in the Lord. He calls on the root doctor simply as a matter of extra security for what it might be worth.

So the organized church and the root doctor have learned to live with one another. Not so the established church and sectarianism. Rural Baptist and Methodist churches especially have had to contend for years with constant defections into one or more of the extreme fundamentalist churches that abound in the South. These churches, whose members are sometimes known as Holy Rollers, usually identify themselves as "Holiness." Frequently, they will use either "Holiness" or "Apostolic" in naming themselves, although they probably have only a loose association, at best, with other similarly named churches. In truth, many of them are not permanent, organized churches at all. They spring up in response to the rousements of some self-anointed evangel, function briefly in any sort of building available, and then break apart over Biblical interpretation or personal disputes among the members. Often such churches dry up when the preacher moves on to another community, another congregation. One of the characteristics of the independent black Holiness churches is that the followers tend to give their loyalty more to the preacher or to his style of preaching or his particular interpretation of the Gospel than to the church as a body. In older, established churches like Saint Stephen, on the other hand, the congregation itself is the continuum force of the church through its lay leadership and its devotion to place and thing. There, for example, the pastor's role is even more restricted than that of a rabbi in the Jewish faith. The pastor is there solely to preach the Gospel, to officiate at weddings, funerals and baptizings and to minister to the congregation's spiritual needs when that ministering is sought. Even if he were the full-time pastor, his position would be a tenuous one.

This competition between establishment churches, as it were, and the Holiness sects was pretty well evenly matched until the great migration out of the cotton and tobacco fields reached its staggering proportion in the 1950s. Then the little Baptist and Methodist churches began to lose ground.

When the migrants poured into the cities, rarely was there a Baptist or a Methodist church to welcome them and pull them into its loving embrace. If they went looking for a church, they found that they could no more be assimilated into the religious life of the urban areas than they could melt into the city's social and economic affairs. Thus, they became more than ever susceptible to the evangelistic fervor of the cult preachers. Some of these preachers were little more than charming mountebanks and glib charlatans, of course. But not all of them. Some were men of genuine good will, who drifted into preaching out of deep religious conviction or a sudden "call" to the ministry after a soul-searing moment of salvation from the life of a sinner to the life of a dedicated churchgoer. To such men it is not enough that they be good Christians, good followers. They must lead other men into the faith, and so they become preachers. They may be ignorant of the Bible and barely able to read. But that is rarely an insurmountable handicap. The important thing is to develop an interpretation of the Gospel and deliver it forcefully, for the followers more often than not are concerned less with the preacher's words than with his delivery and his pulpit manner.

Whatever else is true of these Holiness preachers and their churches, it must be said ultimately that they filled a need in a great many cases when no other church was interested in doing it or capable of doing it. The millions of migrants who poured into the nation's large cities after World War II were churchless as well as homeless. They were cut adrift from all their familiar and necessary moorings. When the nation's religious establishment finally roused itself to that fact and began setting up inner-city ministries, the effort came significantly late. In several urban areas, the Holiness sects had already become institutionalized and so abundant that the migrants of the 1960s were proselytized almost on a block-by-block basis in some of the black ghettos of the Northeast.

Indeed, the black man today often does not have to wait for his arrival in the North. He finds himself converted by Northern-based ghetto churches even before he leaves the South. The cultlike fundamentalism that was barely holding its own in the South found fertile soil in the Northern ghettos, and now it is being exported back to the South stronger than ever. In the little tenant shacks across the South today, it is not at all unusual to find a black family holding Sunday-morning worship service, of sorts, around the kitchen table—listening faithfully to the regular broadcast of one or another of the myriad sectarian preachers who reach vast audiences from home bases in Washington or Baltimore, Philadelphia or Newark. Periodically, these families in the South will band together and charter buses for weekend pilgrimages to one of the Northern temples for special services, singing conventions or simply a Sunday visit. This long-distance worship has created some unusual practices.

Geanie Perry, who lives less than a mile from Saint Stephen's, drives about 4,000 miles a month in his capacity as an elder, or preacher, in the Holiness faith.

In the mid-1950s, Elder Perry, who was not an elder then, migrated to Baltimore. He got saved in a Holiness church, and soon after that he founded his own church in Baltimore, the Apostolic Faith Church of God, Inc. When Elder Perry decided to return to Warren County several years ago, he kept his Baltimore congregation intact. Now he spends one week each month in Baltimore and preaches at another church in Centerville, just beyond Shocco Creek in Franklin County. He also does regular revival work and a little bit of farming when he has time.

It is difficult to overestimate the importance of sectarianism in the lives of the black poor—whether the assessment is made in the North or the South. In the North, even when every other barrier has been swept aside, the deep-rooted religious practices in the ghettos will remain a formidable wall between the races—one that might bar future generations of ghetto blacks from effective assimilation into full community life.

To the extent that it affects the lives of a great many black people and also society at large, the essential point that must be considered in the phenomenon of black sectarianism is this: it represents a retreat into the mindless comfort of the Biblical Gospel at a time when the traditionalist black churches—even some of the fundamentalist churches—are beginning to preach the Social Gospel. The Holiness preacher too often implores his followers to shun the secular world, to suffer now and wait for the peace hereafter. Increasingly, the traditional black churches and a few of the more enlightened Holiness preachers are teaching their followers to move out into the world, to live not just for the hereafter but also for the here and now.

The black revolution of today has moved away from the religious flavor that characterized the early stages of its precursor, the civil-rights movement. Still, the local black church remains the physical headquarters and often the spiritual fountain for social activists in hundreds of black communities across the South. The churches that take seriously their secular responsibility to the community look upon the drift toward religious cultism not merely as a loss of membership and financial support to the established church, but, more important, a wasteful diffusion of black strength in the field of social action.

That is one of the many reasons why Ernest Turner, a strong activist, is more than a little concerned when a black in Warren County—especially one of the members from Saint Stephen—decides to go North. Creola is not an activist. She is not sophisticated enough to understand fully that part of Ernest's concern. But her love and her faith in her own church, coupled with a certain vague awareness in her mind, made it abundantly clear to her that to turn Holiness would be an awful thing. The problem was to weigh on her heavily in the next several weeks until she found an answer.

Chapter Fifteen

WILLIE DURHAM'S HOUSE

Willie Durham's house at 2912 Thirteenth Street, N.W., had absolutely nothing to distinguish it from all the other row houses in Washington's northwest ghetto in the summer of 1969 except that it was to be the home, for a while at least, of the Alston family from Warren County, North Carolina.

The house is high and narrow, with one turret of windows that would break the monotony of the brick front if all the other houses on the block did not also have an identical turret, the same height and the same narrowness. They are attached to one another by common courses of brickwork, so that the only way to determine where one house ends and the next begins is to look at the short walkways leading to the little front stoops. Willie Durham's house sits in the center of the block between Harvard Street and Columbia Road, one house away from the alley that breaks the row construction.

Outside, the house looks only tired. Inside, it seems to be totally exhausted. The front door is recessed slightly from the stoop. It leads into a short hallway that opens simultaneously onto the dining room, at the end, and, to the right, a living room that runs back toward the front of the house. Both rooms seem almost to be one because of the large archway between them. On the right wall of the dining room, a doorway opens onto a short hall leading to the kitchen and back porch, and in the middle of the dining-room wall there are two steps leading up to a small landing, where the stairway turns upward. The second floor has three rooms and a bath, each opening off a common narrow hall, and the third floor has two rooms and a bath.

The front door is held shut only by a hand-turned safety lock. The interior's once fancy woodwork has been covered beyond recognition by successive layers of paint and dirt. The plaster walls are cracked and peeling. The house is dimly lit and perfumed with the lingering sweat of many tenants. The dining room does not function as a dining room any more. When Willie Durham bought the house in 1966, with insurance money collected from an accident on the job, he bought the meager furnishings that went with it. The dining room already had been converted into sleeping quarters when Willie became the owner; because he intended to rent the house, he left the cot in the dining room, reasoning that the more sleeping space he could provide the better his chance would be of keeping the house rented. An old carpet remained on the living-room floor, but elsewhere the floors were bare or covered with ancient linoleum.

Willie Durham believes the house came into his possession by an act of God Almighty—a reward of sorts for six decades of hard work and at least three decades of faithful labor in the holy vineyards. But sometimes Willie wonders if maybe the Lord helped him get the house only as a means of testing his faith. The house has been a source of mighty temptation. Since he became a man of affluence, a man with a house to rent, an upright, God-fearing man who cannot abide sinners, Willie feels constantly put upon by sinners. He had expected the house to give him a comfortable retirement. Now he still had to work part-time to supplement his Social Security because the house was bringing in barely enough to make the payments. Somehow he just could not keep decent people living in the house.

Back home in North Carolina, Willie Durham is known as a hustler, and he is fairly well known in Franklin and Warren counties, although he left Franklin County more than thirty years ago. His reputation as a hustler—a man who works two or three jobs at a time to get ahead in life—is based on his recruiting efforts. Willie is a recruiter with a missionary zeal. He believes that every black man in the South ought to get off the farm as soon as he can, and Willie has done more than one man's share to put that belief into practice. In thirty-two years, he has personally hauled hundreds of men and families out of the rural areas of Franklin and Warren counties into urban areas farther north—first into Norfolk, where he went originally, and then into Washington. Regularly, he has made six to eight trips a year back to North Carolina, picking up men and introducing them to employers in the city. Willie goes more often than that sometimes, when employers have an especially critical need for workers. Willie has hauled as many as seven men northward on a single trip.

When he bought the house on Thirteenth Street, Willie figured he would not have a bit of trouble keeping it rented. He knew from his recruiting hauls that people coming up from the South would have appreciated it if he could have offered them a place to live. But it had not worked out that way at all. It seemed to Willie Durham that he had been plagued by nothing but sinners and deadbeats ever since he started renting the house. If there was anything Willie Durham could not abide, it was sinners and deadbeats.

Willie had joined a Holiness church soon after leaving the farm as a young man, and over the years he had developed his faith to the extent that it dominated him totally. He had done some lay preaching, and his conversation—any conversation—tended to sound like a sermon. His faith was so exclusively his that he tended to be intolerant of anyone of less faith or a different faith. Anyone who does not subscribe to the Holiness faith is a sinner in Willie Durham's judgment—and that includes his family. All other churches, no matter what they practice or how devout they might be, are sham churches—"sinner churches," he calls them.

Willie Durham's religious fervor was one reason why

the house was only partially rented when the Alstons moved to Washington, one reason why the house was less clean than it might have been otherwise. Previous tenants had tended to depart hurriedly and in anger.

If there was little else to recommend it, though, at least the house in the summer of 1969 was whole. That block of Thirteenth Street has no business houses, and so it escaped the mob fury that roiled around it during the Washington rioting of April 1968. A block away, chilling evidence of the rioting remained more than a year later, and Creola began noticing it after they left downtown Washington, heading north on Fourteenth Street. At first she gave it only casual attention. But boarded-up windows changed to vacant windows as Wiley drove deeper into the ghetto—vacant windows in shells of gutted buildings, windows that showed blue sky through them as Creola looked up from the car.

"The house is just around the corner yonder," Wash said as Wiley turned right at the Harvard Street intersection. And Creola suddenly felt a shiver of fear then, realizing for the first time that her family would be living so close to these fire-blackened walls, these half-standing monuments to the misery and anger that the city can produce in the breasts of its people.

Fourteenth Street had been busy with Saturday-afternoon shoppers and numberless, aimless little knots of men and women and youngsters, who seemed not to mind the steamy heat of the street. But the June sun lay heavy and undisturbed on Thirteenth Street except for an occasional car and three or four listless children playing under the scrawny tree at the mouth of the alley just beyond Willie Durham's house. The block seemed almost deserted in comparison with the bustle a street away.

Wiley turned into the alley and then backed out so that he could park against the southbound curb in front of the house. For a moment Creola worried because she did not see Willie Durham's Dodge. But Wash told her Willie probably had parked back in the alley at the rear of the house. Even as he said it, Creola saw George, her twelve-year-old, dash out the door to meet them at the car. Everybody in Willie Durham's car had been there an hour, George said.

Now Robert and the smaller children came running out of the house to greet the new arrivals. Creola handed the baby to Bernice and quickly shook off the fatigue of being cramped in the car during the long drive. With all of her brood about her again she felt good now. The whole family was laughing and talking as the children pulled their mother up the walkway. The Alston children had never had a bathroom in their own home. The little ones, too small for school, were only vaguely familiar with indoor plumbing. Martha, sixteen and the oldest girl, was the only one not laughing. She was still scared, she said, from Willie Durham's driving on the superhighway. That man had scared her half to death, she said.

A man and a woman Creola did not know were sitting in the partial shade of the stoop, and Creola smiled and called hello to them as she and Wash and the children started up the steps. The man and the woman stared and smiled briefly. But they did not move as Creola stepped by them.

"That's the other fellow living here." Wash said

when they were inside the door. "Him and his wife live on the third floor. They won't be no bother to us."

Creola was not sure about that. Both of them, she had noticed, were drinking beer.

Willie Durham was standing on the landing off the dining room, where the stairway started, when Wash and Creola walked in. He gave them a moment or two to look over the two front rooms and then stepped down to the first step, so that he stood close to the family gathered about him but still slightly above them, the way a preacher might stand on a small pulpit.

Willie hitched up his baggy trousers and removed his half-rim glasses to clean them. In the poor light of the room it looked for a moment as if he might have three eyes—two small seeing eyes, and a smaller, unseeing third eye in the middle of his forehead. The effect was created by the presence of a tiny round indentation carved by the impact of a bullet fired into his skull several years earlier during a domestic argument. Willie Durham and his family have been separated ever since. But Willie and his bullet never parted company. The doctor who treated him decided to leave the bullet where it had lodged.

With his glasses safely back on his nose, Willie Durham gave one more hitch to his trousers and then cleared his throat to call for attention. He wanted the Alstons to know just how fortunate they were and how glad Willie Durham was to have them in his house and what Willie Durham expected of people who lived there. His house, he said, belonged partly to God because Willie Durham had got it through and by God Almighty's help.

"God suffered me to get this house," he said. "And some way and somehow he makes arrangements at the ends of the months for me to make the payments. Yeah. If I had been a servant of the Devil, I would have been out of this house. People told me when I bought this house I wouldn't keep it six months. Said I'd be out of here in six months."

Willie went on to tell how he had moved people out, how he had refused to rent to some people even, because they were sinners. He did not want to rent to sinner people—people who cuss, smoke, drink liquor, and say their funny words and do what they want to do and think they are going to see God. He would not rent his house to people like that, he said.

Willie talked for maybe fifteen minutes, pausing regularly at the end of each complete thought to mull over what he had just said. During each of these pauses Willie would stare intently at the far wall of the dining room, or he would look about him from one wall to another or from one piece of furniture to another. His face would have about it a vague, puzzled frown—a look that seemed to indicate an agony of groping for the next complete thought or partial thought, of trying to recall just what the last thought was. He spoke in short, choppy sentences—sometimes incomplete sentences and sometimes fragmentary thoughts or snatches of Biblical phrases. Often during the pauses, he would unconsciously repeat his last spoken phrase. More often, he bridged the gaps in the monologue with a soft, rhythmical "uh huh" or a "yeah." He also frequently announced the discovery of the next thought with another "yeah," spoken with a different expression. Strangely, though,

Willie Durham's House

Willie's "uh huhs" and "yeahs" were expressive and communicative—more so at times than his full sentences, because he had developed a good range of inflections.

By the time Willie Durham had finished talking, Creola had decided that she did not like him. She thought he used God's name too loosely, proclaimed his religion too loudly. As Wash and Willie Durham took her through the house, she wondered whether they had made a mistake in moving to Washington, whether living in this man's house would work out.

The Alstons were renting only part of the house. They were to have the entire first floor plus two rooms and the bath on the second floor. The couple *upstairs* rented the entire third floor plus one of the second-floor rooms, which had been converted to a kitchen. Willie Durham was going to fix up the basement and live there himself. But Wash explained to Creola that Willie would have to stay on the main floor until he could get the basement fixed up. Willie would sleep on the old sofa in the living room. Wash assured Creola that Willie Durham was a good man and that he would not be any problem. The Alstons would be paying ninety-five dollars a month in rent. Creola thought that was pretty high. But it did include heat and lights, and Wash did have a good salary now.

It was the sight of Bernice a few minutes later that snapped Creola out of her own doubt and gathering gloom about the house and the city. Bernice was sitting on the stairway landing after the family had made a tour of the first and second floors. She was almost shivering, rocking slightly back and forth and hugging little

Hosea to her breast. The look in Bernice's face clearly told Creola that Bernice was unhappy. At once, Creola's own attitude changed. Suddenly she realized that she almost had let her family down. If they were to be able to expect any reasonable amount of happiness in the new home, Creola knew, she would have to show happiness herself.

She began smiling, and her voice sounded strong and positive when she delivered to the family her assessment. "A little paint here and a little fixing-up there," she said, "and it'll be home. All it needs is a woman's touch."

After that, everything went better. Creola sent the boys to bring in the family's few possessions from the cars. Bernice was told to look out for the little children. Martha was to help her mother in the kitchen. They would eat the picnic food now. Later, Creola and Wash would do some shopping, and they all would have a hot dinner before bed.

The family celebrated the beginning of its new life that night with a dinner of fried chicken, and then Creola assigned bed space for everyone. Martha and Bernice were to have the big bed upstairs. Four-year-old Emily would sleep on a pallet next to the bed, and the three little boys—seven-year-old Douglas, six-year-old Aaron and three-year-old Michael—would sleep on the mattress on the floor. George and ten-year-old Robert would sleep on the cot in the dining room. The cot really was not wide enough for both of them, but it would have to do until Wash could go back home for the furniture. Willie Durham would be in later, and he would sleep on the sofa in the living room. Until they got Hosea's crib, he would sleep in the bed with Creola and Wash.

Creola's mind was troubled and her prayer was long when she knelt at the bed that night. "Heavenly Father," she said, "we thank you for guiding us to a safe destination. Help us to accept this place as our home and help us to make it a good home if it is God's will that it is to be our home. If it is not God's will, then give us the courage to endure and take things as they come."

As usual, she prayed that Wash would someday come to know the joy she knew of loving God, of being in His presence and of talking with Him. She prayed for her children's safety in the city and for God's hand to help her guide them and protect them. She prayed for the people back home. She asked God to guide her to a good church in the city. She prayed some more about the house and finished by asking God to forgive her for her thoughts about Willie Durham.

Her prayer ended, Creola rose and looked at her baby and her husband, and it occurred to her in that happy moment that this was Saturday night—the first Saturday night in a very long time that Wash had not taken a drink. In that moment she was so happy she had to cry.

Chapter Sixteen
THE GREAT MIGRATION

Donnie Gibson and the Alstons and the Fantastic Four were but tiny specks in one of the turgid streams of human migration flowing out of the nation's hinterlands in the summer of 1969. They were, in the fullest sense, the flotsam and jetsam of society's determined march toward the Good Life. Unknowingly, they and tens of thousands like them had become a part of the greatest movement of human beings in history—America's rural-to-urban migration.

During the past thirty years, about 30,000,000 people have left the nation's farms and rural small towns for urban life. This silent, deep-running flow of migrants rolled on unassisted, undirected and largely unnoticed —bleeding the countryside of its most valuable resource and bloating the cities with former tenant farmers, displaced hillbillies and young blacks running from nothing to nothing.

They left the dust bowl of Oklahoma, the grainfields of Iowa, coves and hollows of the Southern Appalachians and, most important today, the cotton and tobacco fields of the South.

They fled hunger and poverty and servitude, just as the 600,000 souls of that first great Exodus fled penury and bondage. The latter-day exodus, too, sought the land of milk and honey.

The Great Migration

But the modern exodus has had no voice from a burning bush, no pillars of cloud and fire to guide it, no Moses to lead it, no prophets to chronicle it and wrap it in Biblical reverence. It did not go unrecorded. The nation's sociologists and economic planners knew it. The governmental bureaucracy faithfully documented and plotted it with charts and graphs and impressive statistics. The bibliography alone of published works on the migration of farm people from 1946 through 1960 covers thirty-five pages of a U.S. Department of Agriculture publication.

Still, the nation as a whole did not know it—or, knowing it, refused to be concerned about it. America was geared to production and consumption and ever-bigger growth. Progress was the thing—progress and prosperity and production. And America produced and prospered and grew richer. Society marched onward and upward, fighting wars abroad and imagined Communist revolutions at home, and largely ignoring the makings of a real revolution. The United States was and is a nation on the make because it is a collection of people on the make. Civic boosterism could not admit to the problems of the poor and the dispossessed; so the silent, swollen streams of migrants flowed on.

West of the Mississippi, the migrants went out to California if they were young or if they could make it that far. If they had families, the migrants moved out of the small towns and the farm areas into large cities like Houston or Denver. Some of them looked north and east to the Chicago area. If they were white, they could travel only 100 or 200 miles and find a city and a job. If they were black or if they began their journey in the

South, they went farther and their destination and route were determined before they left home; for as surely as fish and fowl follow the same routes year after year in nature's ordained migration, so does the migrating Southerner follow a path tramped out for him during decades of travel by friends and relatives. Many Deep South Negroes go straight to Chicago and the neighboring industrial cities or join the migratory stream of upper South Negroes heading toward the nation's great urban sprawl that begins in Washington and stretches into New England. The Appalachian whites, in general, head into the Ohio Valley and on toward the industrial cities bordering the Great Lakes.

In the beginning, the great migration of the dispossessed farmer was almost heedless flight. The migrant knew only that he was *leaving* a place. He did not think of himself as *going to* a place. Wherever he found a job and a place to live, he established a migration beachhead. And then migration began to breed migration because the first man sent back word to his relatives and his friends: "Come on up. The money's good." And they did come; and then they in turn sent back word to their relatives and their friends. Pretty soon the little rivulets of migration became rivers and then swollen rivers.

As the beachheads expanded into clusters of blacks or hillbillies and then into neighborhoods of them, something began to happen in the cities. The natives began fleeing to new suburbs, and the neighborhoods of migrants became ghettos of migrants—50,000 here, 100,000 there. Entire cities, large and small alike, began assuming new identities because they were experiencing forty and fifty per cent turnovers—and worse—in the kind of people who live in the inner cities.

The migrants poured into the ghettos, often carrying with them little more than the clothes on their backs and the hope and the fear and the misery in their souls. For solace, the whites took with them their guitars and their mournful music. The blacks took their religion and their blackness.

The migrant streams flowed on, and periodically the sociologists and demographers measured the depth and strength of the streams and wrote learned papers about it that were read by other sociologists and demographers. Most Americans did not pay much attention to the migration because there seemed nothing of importance in it. The United States, after all, is a nation of movers. Everybody moves at one time or another. It is a part of our heritage and our modern psyche as a people on the make. The attitude is: What the hell! If we had not been a nation of movers, we never would have conquered the western frontier. To move means to look for opportunity, and opportunity often means moving. If a man cannot make it in one place, he moves to another place. It is as simple as that.

The migrant streams flowed on and the strongest, the smartest, the best-educated, the most ambitious of the migrants—maybe half of them—were absorbed productively and disappeared into the great middle class. In the beginning the cities digested even the least able. But finally, a few years ago, the cities began to explode from indigestion, and the nation came to suspect that migration was not that simple after all. Americans finally began to see the huge urban ghettos for what they are—a kind of Fifth Circle of the Inferno seething with self-destructive anger. The nation began also to understand that the hopelessness of the ghetto really began in the hopelessness of the backwoods South; that half a century of migration, directly and indirectly, is a root cause of many of the nation's deepest problems: hunger, poverty, crime, social unrest, personal alienation.

In his native milieu of the rural South, the black is a gentle, peace-loving man. He is slow to anger, even when another man's thumb is pressing him down and pushing him off the land. Denied a realistic choice of where he shall live, how he shall earn a meager living, he becomes an unwilling migrant, and still he cannot rise to anger. He leaves the land in a welter of emotions —he is frustrated and confused and disheartened. He might feel aggrieved. But he is not angry. His strongest feelings, as he arrives in the city on the migratory stream, are fear and hope. Usually he overcomes the fear. Too often he loses the hope, and then anger begins to eat at him. At some indeterminate point after he reaches the city—it might be three years or five years or ten years—the once gentle man of the soil becomes the angry man of the ghetto. It does not happen to all the migrants, of course. Some make it out of the ghetto. Some remain in the ghetto, half dead and half alive, wasting life away in a mindless wallow of despair. Others are able to remain there and still somehow achieve a satisfaction in their lives. There is, after all, a womblike warmth and security in the ghetto for some of its inhabitants.

But the migrant streams that began running full during the labor shortage of World War I are relentless. Every year, they pour another million or so people into the cities. Every year, the man who arrived in the ghetto last year finds himself crowded even more in the competition for decent jobs and decent housing. Pretty soon, the migrant does not think of himself as a migrant any more. He is a resident. The migrant is the fresh arrival, and the former migrant begins to resent him, even to despise him, because the fresh arrival, in his desperate need for work, will lower wages and thereby drive down the wages for others; in his immediate need for housing, he will pay too much and pack in too many people to help share the rent. For some earlier migrants, the new migrant is a constant reminder of something—a way of life, a former status—that he wants to put behind him.

Chapter Seventeen
THE WANDERERS

When will it all end? When will the migrant streams dry up? When will the cities get at least a respite? There is some evidence now that the exodus from the farms has dropped considerably from its level of the 1940s and 1950s. Indeed, it *had* to slow down eventually, because the birth rate, even in the most fecund rural areas, could not go on matching the rate of out-migration—especially when the migration was cutting steadily into the rural population of childbearing age. It would seem, on the surface at least, that out-migration from many parts of the nation has petered out for an obvious reason: some of the rural areas have been bled dry. Migration has scraped down to the bottom of the barrel, leaving only the old folks and the few landed gentry. How many ex-farmers are left to migrate out of Colorado, for example, when the state's entire farm population ten years ago had been depleted to the point where it was only slightly more than seven per cent of the state's over-all population? How many potential out-migrants can Madison County, North Carolina, muster after four decades of steady decimation—four decades in which the county's sinew, the men and women between eighteen and forty-five, left to pull society's plow in more fertile fields?

The answer is not as obvious as it might seem. The potential out-migration from the tobacco fields of the coastal-plains region alone is around a quarter of a million black people in the coming decade. It could well be greater. The figure probably is smaller for the white out-migrants from the Southern Appalachians. But in both areas, and in the Deep South as well, an optimistic appraisal of current migration is misleading because of two important factors that have been either overlooked or underestimated in some studies of the problem.

The out-migrants of previous years have tended to replace themselves in some rural areas by sending youngsters back home to live with relatives through high school or until they drop out of school and migrate themselves. It is doubtful whether even the United States Census Bureau has been able to make an accurate

The Wanderers

head count of these youngsters, for they are constantly being shuttled back and forth between parents in the North and grandparents in the South. In the Gibson family, for example, Otis and Julia raised seven children and saw six of them migrate to the North. On the surface, it would seem that the Gibsons' contribution to the migratory streams had ended. But the six sons and daughters who went North have sent back six grandchildren—potential out-migrants a decade or so from now.

The second factor is that the nature of migration has changed noticeably within the past decade. Once, there were two kinds of migrants: the "migrant worker," a man who moved constantly from one region of the nation to another following agriculture crops, a true nomad; and the "permanent out-migrant," the man who quit one place to take up permanent residence in another. The migrant workers tend to remain constantly in farm work, although they peel off occasionally into low-level industrial jobs. The permanent out-migrants, as they apply to the nation's social ills, tend to leave agriculture permanently for other jobs in urban areas.

It was once possible to make a clear distinction between the two groups. But now many of the out-migrants who once would have been classified as permanent have become almost nomadic. You do not have to look very hard to see the extent of this nomadism. There is evidence of it aplenty in almost any mountain hollow in the Southern Appalachians, almost any tobacco field in the coastal plains. In some rural communities it is hard to find even one adult who has not been North at least once, often a dozen or more times.

They go North, but they cannot or will not stay more than a few months. They find work, but they cannot make an adjustment to the city. They either lose their jobs or quit them, and return home on the slightest pretext. These pathetic souls thus have become truly stateless, even homeless, wanderers because they cannot live in the city and they cannot earn a living at home. They are pulled constantly back and forth, first by an economic need and then by some, even more basic, homing instinct.

In some Southern Appalachian areas, twice-a-year migration has become a routine way of life. The migrants leave the South in early winter and take an industrial job somewhere in the North. In the spring, when the pull of the land becomes irresistible, the migrants move back to the fields and hollows to make a small crop, work somebody else's, or simply to take what work is available at home. Almost routinely, too, the whites from the Southern mountains will apply for unemployment compensation—surprisingly often they will qualify. The blacks have not yet discovered the widespread possibilities of it—at least, they have not developed it to the extent that whites have. Blacks more often fall back on the less lucrative but more permanent benefits of public welfare.

And for every out-migrant who returns to the South, there is likely to be at least one who hopes to return. These unwilling expatriates are sensible enough to know that there is no reason to return South until some way opens up for a man to make a living. So they remain in the North, plodding through one day at a time, sometimes forging good careers, but still pining—aching—to go home again. They go back for holidays and graduations so that they can keep friendships and dreams alive, feel the land, smell the crops, hear the croak of frogs and the song of a bobwhite at dusk. They go back to renew themselves. And then they turn on the switch again and re-enter the world of push. Often they go back North with a new purpose: to pay for a little piece of land in the South or, if they own the land already, to start saving toward the price of a trailer home or a little retirement house.

The exiles have a fast and effective system of keeping up with the news from back home. This was demonstrated clearly in the reaction to an incident in 1969. Floyd McKissick, a North Carolina native and former national chairman of the Congress of Racial Equality, announced early in the year that he and several associates had bought 1,800 acres of land in Warren County. The land would be developed as the home of a new city—black-inspired and black-developed—to be called "Soul City." Soul City would provide jobs and housing for an ultimate population of 18,000 people in an area where out-migration had been extremely heavy owing to the lack of decent jobs and decent housing.

The news electrified former Warren County black people across the nation. Immediately, Ernest Turner's mail began to include letters like the one from a supermarket manager in Washington who had left Warren County eight years earlier. He listed his background and qualifications—business school and company training after leaving Warren County—and ended with a plea to Ernest Turner. The man wanted to come home and go into the supermarket business in Soul City. Although Ernest Turner had nothing to do with the development of Soul City, he received several letters like this. McKissick's mail was flooded with such pleas; he also received personal visits.

One of the purposes in developing Soul City is to stop the out-migration—to turn it around, even, so that out-migrants can come home again. If he ever did have any doubts about whether his idea was sound, McKissick does not now. A subsequent block-by-block survey of sections of Harlem turned up hundreds of former Southerners eager to move into Soul City and willing to undergo job-training programs, if necessary, to get there.

Within a year McKissick had moved four house trailers onto the rolling pasture land to house an office and a resident staff, and planning and development work alone had created about sixty new jobs for black people in the area. McKissick had commitments from several industries and businesses to build in Soul City, and he was exploring a possible training and relocation program with an organization called Manpower Development Corporation of Chapel Hill. Manpower Development is an outgrowth of a poverty agency that won permanence and enough status to get the official blessing of the staid National Association of Manufacturers. Besides its work on the Soul City project, Manpower Development has been trying other methods to stem the migration out of the region and to redirect the migratory streams so that they run not into the urban ghettos of the North but, rather, into the small urban centers of the state and the region—areas where there is a critical labor shortage. One of its projects is a deliberate effort to create new beachheads of migration by recruiting ex-farm workers out of the labor-surplus area of the coastal plains and moving them into the labor-shortage area of the industrial Piedmont section of the Carolinas.

One of the difficult things about migration is that once a migratory stream cuts its path it stubbornly resists redirection. Thus, the paradox that exists in the upper South today. At the same time that thousands of black people are being forced off the land in the coastal-plains region for lack of work, there exists—sometimes less than 200 miles away—a critical labor shortage. Ironically, the labor shortage in the Piedmont region exists mostly in textiles, construction, services, and other low-skill, low-wage jobs—jobs that would provide the potential out-migrants with as good a real income as they could find in the urban ghettos of the North, and a more familiar way of life. Yet, the migrants continue going North along the familiar routes largely because that is the way a brother or a sister or an uncle or a cousin has gone before; because a relative will be waiting at the end of the line.

This paradox in the regional labor market was not lost on the textile industry, although it has been slow to acknowledge and accept the alternatives open to it—raising wages to compete for available white labor or hiring blacks and training them, if necessary, to man the looms and spinning frames. The mills began hiring blacks a few years ago, owing to federal pressure and their own economic plight, and that experience led to something that may someday be regarded as a significant turning point in the nation's rural-to-urban migration as well as in the textile industry.

The upper South got its first great industrial base around the turn of the century, when the textile industry began moving south from New England into the Piedmont region of the Carolinas and Georgia. The Piedmont is a narrow swath paralleling the Southern Appalachian Mountains between the coastal plains on the east and the Appalachian foothills on the west. Its red clay soil never was suitable for profitable farming, but its rivers rushing toward the fall line were ideal for development of industrial power. The textile industry found advantages in nearness to the cotton crops plus a native labor force that would put a song in any robber baron's heart—a people so fiercely independent, so resistant to the courtship of organized labor, that they became absolutely pliant as workers.

The workers remain tame even today. Cotton has long since moved, first farther south and then west. But textiles have stayed on permanently. Soon after the industry moved south, the Piedmont section of the Carolinas became the textile center of the nation. It remains so even today, although perhaps not for much longer. The textile industry has within the past few years begun to move into the coastal-plains region to find the labor it cannot get any longer in the bustling, competitive Piedmont. One company alone—Burlington Industries, the nation's largest textile firm—operates twenty-three textile plants in the plains region of the two Carolinas, employing about 11,300 persons. It put into the area a capital investment of $125 million in the decade of the sixties, including seven plants.

Local and state governments cooperate with new industry willingly, for the most part, offering tax advantages, utilities, sometimes even free land and virtually free buildings. One of the more significant steps by government is a huge industrial training center begun in 1969 in Williamsburg County, South Carolina, Donnie Gibson's home county. The Williamsburg Regional Manpower Center was built specifically to take advantage of the moving itch among textilists and to encourage them and other industries to relocate in the region. Eventually, the center is expected to turn out about 3,000 graduates a year on a supermarket approach toward education. The students—of all ages and all kinds of educational background—will enter through one door and several months or years later, leave through another door, with training that will range anywhere from basic adult education to rather sophisticated technical skills. The premise is that work will be available somewhere in the region by then because of new jobs being created now.

But just as the migratory streams are not as simple as they seem, neither is the effort to stop them or redirect them. At best, it will likely be another five years or more before there are any significant results. Unless human nature and the prevailing social philosophy change drastically within the region, the first fruits of industrial development will be plucked by whites rather than blacks. In some communities, the white power structure plainly does not want new industry. In others, the ruling elders would not mind at all if things rocked along as they are until 3,000 or 4,000 more blacks leave.

In Warren County, North Carolina, the responsibility for industrial development rests in the hands of a paid director whose social philosophy is a marvel of nineteenth-century perfection—a true and beautiful piece of antiquity, created in a plantation economy and preserved and handed down unprofaned through the generations. One of the men who sells bus tickets to migrants leaving Warrenton, the county seat, would rather sell them a one-way ticket than a round-trip. He looks upon the migrants as people who "go back and forth like birds. Some make five and six trips a year. Their parents live up there on welfare and they stay down here, living on welfare and going to school at public expense. They spend more money on bus tickets back and forth than it would take to support 'em down here."

And so the migrant streams roll on. And so they will continue to roll on, pouring into the cities far too many men of the soil and plow, the pick and shovel; men forced out of the fields and hollows into urban pressure pots that baffle and beat down other men far better equipped for urban survival.

The high-school graduates will go right on boarding northbound buses and trains still wearing their graduation clothes, and fresh in the knowledge that society has deceived them. Society tells black high-school students that they are educated, knowing very well that they are not. Society implies, but no longer says it outright, that the diploma is negotiable in the labor market. But that same local society says no from behind its desk when the black graduate makes the job-hunting round.

So the youngsters say to hell with it, and the old people hang on. They hang on from one crop to another, praying and hoping and growing steadily more feeble and deeper in debt, until the day when the landlord cuts them loose or the supply merchant refuses credit—or a friend or relative or professional recruiter comes by and says, Man, you've got to move.

Chapter Eighteen
ROCHESTER

In 1929, two brothers named Hal and George F. Fish drove from their home in Middletown, New York, to Sanford, Florida, on a celery-buying trip. They decided to rent some land in Sanford and grow celery there because they already were farming in Wayne County, New York, and the Florida operation would give them almost a year-round growing season.

One of the farm hands they hired in Florida was a black man named John Gibson. Gibson apparently was a good employee, for in the summer of 1931 the brothers Fish sent for him to work the harvest of their New York farm. They asked Gibson to recruit a crew of field hands and bring them along. Nearly forty years later, when a newspaper reporter began tracing to its genesis the migration of black people into the Rochester area, John Gibson, of Sanford, Florida, could chuckle and tell the reporter, "It started from me."

According to Gibson's account, which appeared in the Rochester *Times-Union* in March 1969, there was scarcely more than a handful of black families living in the rural communities around Rochester when he first went there. Gibson and his crew seldom saw other blacks living in the area. The farm crops were harvested by the men who owned the land or by white labor hired on a temporary basis. In the city itself, there might have been a few other black families. But not many had settled that far north because there had been little demand for their labor.

Year after year, Gibson returned with a new crew of farm workers. He would recruit them in the Sanford area, take them to New York around midsummer, when the harvest season was pretty well ended in Florida, and then take them back to Florida in late fall. But sometimes Gibson went back with fewer men because some had flaked off from the migrant stream to take permanent jobs in the Rochester area. The demand for migrant labor increased steadily over the years, and by 1937 John Gibson was hauling two crews of men northward every season, recruiting not only in Florida but also at stops along the way in Georgia and the Carolinas. And still he was taking fewer men back every year. For every load of twenty-five or thirty on the northbound trip, there were six or eight or ten who did not return South. They stayed, and eventually they sent for relatives. Their numbers increased to the extent that somebody in Rochester in later years could coin a new word for the English language—a word to describe the migrant who stayed: "staygrant."

Eventually, the demand for migrant farm labor diminished. But the flow of migrants did not. It grew—gradually at first, then more rapidly, and always steadily. In 1950, the nonwhite population of Monroe County, which had been only a beachhead for black migrants twenty years earlier, was nearly 8,000. The nonwhite designation meant chiefly black, and most of them were living not throughout the county but in the city of Rochester. And then technology, birth rates and the cumulative effect of two decades of moving and staying began to flood Rochester with more Southern migrants than it could absorb. From 1950 to 1960, the county's nonwhite population, still mostly in the city, jumped to 24,184—an increase in ten years of 208.8 per cent. Five years later, it had climbed to about 35,000, and the city's Bureau of Municipal Research was estimating a nonwhite population of 45,000 by 1970.

Rioting in the summer of 1964 jerked the city awake to the population crisis that had been so long abuilding. When Rochester began a self-assessment, it found that it was really two cities—one of them a nether world of black people existing within the main city and yet not really part of it. White Rochester had high employment, high income and a high standard of living. Black Rochester was a city of high unemployment and higher underemployment. While white Rochester was going up, black Rochester was going down in everything except the number of people and the measure of their problems.

Perhaps to a greater extent than any other American city, Rochester accurately assessed its problems and adequately marshaled its resources to meet them. Still, Rochester could no more stem the flow of migrants than any other city. It could identify the migrant streams and define them. By far the largest number of in-migrants was coming from the area around Sanford, Florida. The second largest stream originated in Williamsburg County, S.C. Between them, the two Southern localities accounted for the majority of the city's black population.

Rochester could, and did, attempt to influence the flow of migrants between Sanford and Rochester. At the suggestion of Rochester School Superintendent Herman R. Goldberg, Governors Nelson Rockefeller of New York and Claude Kirk of Florida set up a "New York–Florida interstate opportunities panel" to examine the migrant flow. By the summer of 1969, the informal compact had produced an agreement by the two states to swap information on industrial development, and brought about a one-year teacher exchange between a high school in Rochester and one in Sanford, but not much else.

Neither Rochester nor Sanford nor the two governors had appreciably changed the migrant streams by the Thursday afternoon in July when Amos Jones and Elijah Scott arrived at the Trailways bus station in Rochester. But the city's two newest in-migrants did have one advantage over many of those of a few years earlier, and over some 1969 migrants arriving in other cities: a job of some sort was almost a certainty.

Chapter Nineteen
THE FANTASTIC TWO

Amos's brother Herman was waiting at the bus station when Amos and Elijah arrived in Rochester. Herman had called his mother Wednesday to learn when Amos was leaving. Then he had called the station to find out when the bus would get in.

Amos did not see Herman at first. But then he recognized the voice as Herman came up from behind. "Hey, man. Where are you going?" Herman said.

Amos was glad to see him. "What you doing here?" he asked. "How'd you know what time we'd get in?"

Herman explained and then asked about the trip.

"Oh, man. My butt's sore," Amos said. "But it was a pretty good trip, except for the layover in Washington."

They had got into Washington about 11:00 the night before and had to wait about three hours for the Rochester bus. It was a hard three hours. They got a hamburger, and then flipped through a couple of magazines and walked around the station for a while. They must have gone to the bathroom a dozen times, and they finally ended up just sitting and trying to stay awake.

Once when Elijah went to the men's room, a man came up beside him kind of secretlike and asked if Elijah wanted to buy a ring.

"What kind of ring?" Elijah asked.

"Diamond ring," the man said. "Engagement ring for your girl."

"Nah. I ain't got a girl," Elijah said.

"Yeah, but see, this is a real good buy. You could sell it to a buddy and make a good profit."

"I got a buddy outside that might want to buy it," Elijah said. "You can talk to him."

With a great display of furtiveness, the man showed Amos the set of rings—an engagement ring and a matching wedding band. The set was worth at least $300, the man said. But Amos could have both rings for $40.

"Why you selling so cheap?" Amos asked.

To tell the truth, the man said, he had stolen the rings the night Martin Luther King was shot, and had been saving them for his own use someday. But now he needed the money.

Amos really would have liked to own the rings—at least the engagement ring. A ring like that might come in handy some time, he thought, if a girl was real stubborn and needed some extra persuasion. But he did not have the money, and the idea of buying stolen property did not appeal to him.

After one more try, the man gave up and went looking for another customer. After he was out of earshot, Amos asked Elijah, "Why'd you bring that guy to me?"

"Man, I was trying to get rid of him," Elijah said, laughing.

On the bus to Rochester, they had kept hoping at every stop that a good-looking girl would get on—one traveling alone. They kidded each other about who would get first choice at romancing her. But none did, and they talked of old romances. Elijah's mother was living in Rochester—had lived there for several years—and Elijah had visited the city before, so both of them had old girl friends to call on.

The first day in Rochester set a pattern for other days to follow. Herman had moved to another apartment since the previous summer, and they all walked there; it was only three blocks from the bus station, and Herman's wife, Sara Jane, had the car. Amos was surprised to learn that he would have his own room. The new apartment had three bedrooms, and Herman and Sara Jane had only one child, two-year-old Carolyn.

Herman showed the boys around the apartment and then went back to work at the body shop. He told Amos to loaf for a few days. The owner of the shop was out of town until the next week. Herman was sure there would be a job available when the man got back; there would not be any need to apply for a job until then.

When Amos had unpacked and changed clothes, the two of them went to Elijah's mother's house on Thomas Street, stopping long enough for Elijah to say hello and change clothes. It was close to five o'clock before they got on the street. They walked for a while, stopped in a couple of stores, and worked their way gradually to a neighborhood park that Elijah remembered as a good place to meet girls. But they did not meet any that interested them, and they went back to Herman's apartment when the park closed at 8:30. They watched television and talked about friends and good times back in South Carolina, and Amos went to bed early, as soon as Elijah left. He reminded himself that he would have to look up Willie Chandler. But as it turned out, the days came and went, and there never seemed to be enough time to find the address Amos had in his pocket.

The next four days were about like that first day. Amos and Elijah always got together, but nothing much seemed to happen. Friday night, they went to Fifty Acres, and Saturday they went to the drag strip. They met some girls, but nothing special.

Herman took them to work with him Tuesday morning because his boss was back in town. On Herman's recommendation both of them were hired and went to work that day. They would be drawing $105 a week straight time while learning to straighten, sand out and putty-up sheet metal. For Amos, the job lasted six weeks. Herman took Sara Jane and Carolyn back to South Carolina over the Fourth of July vacation; when they got back to Rochester, Herman told Amos he had decided to move. His granddaddy had told Herman about a body shop that had closed in Kingstree. Herman could rent the vacant building for seventy dollars a month. Herman was a good body man, his granddaddy reminded him, and if he came back and really worked at it, he could make himself a good business.

"Mama wants you to come back, too," Herman told Amos.

Amos was not sure he wanted to go back. He had kind of liked living alone while Herman's family was back South. When his mother called a few days later, though, Amos told her he would come back. With Herman gone he would have to pay room and board somewhere, and that would not leave him much money.

Besides, he figured, sometimes you got to listen to old people even when you don't want to.

Two weeks later, after Amos and Herman finished work on a Friday, the family left that night in Herman's Plymouth. They got home Saturday night, and Sunday afternoon Amos stopped at James McClary's house and learned that Ernest Tisdale was back home, too.

Ernest knew from the moment he boarded the bus in Kingstree, the first Monday after school was out, that he would not like living with his brother in Miami. It weighed on him so heavily that he had thought very briefly about just turning around when he got to Miami. That was somewhere in Florida, when the bus had stopped long enough for him to order some bacon and eggs, which did not taste the way bacon and eggs tasted at home. Later, he wondered why he didn't do it, why he didn't just turn around and change buses right there in that town in Florida.

But he did not do it. He had set out for Miami, and he would go to Miami. At 5:30 the next morning, he stepped down from the bus in the Miami station and called his brother to come and get him, not feeling any too good about things. Joe Cecil drove up a few minutes later, and at 8:00 that morning Ernest reported to work as a construction helper at the same place Joe Cecil worked. He put in an eight-hour day. It had started out just about the way Ernest figured it would. Joe Cecil was that way.

Ernest liked his brother well enough. Joe Cecil was a good man. But Ernest and Joe Cecil were different.

Sometimes Ernest wondered what Joe Cecil got out of life. He worked practically all the time because he was trying to save enough money to go back to South Carolina and build a house. When he got off work from the construction job, he came home to eat and then went to work on the night shift at a service station. What time he wasn't working, he most likely was in church.

Joe Cecil's religion was something else that Ernest could not understand. Ernest was about as religious as anybody else who was normal. He went to church most every Sunday and prayed fairly regularly. He tried to live right and do right, and he figured that was what religion was supposed to be. But Joe Cecil was different. Joe Cecil was almost a fanatic on religion. Take smoking, for instance. He didn't believe in it, so Ernest couldn't smoke in the house or in the car going to work or coming from work. The only time he could smoke was on the job or when he went out at night, and there were not many nights when he went out.

Joe Cecil did not approve of running around at night. That was something the poolroom crowd did. Every time they passed the poolroom, Ernest got a lecture about the poolroom crowd that did not work. But Ernest did not really care much about going out at night anyway. He had made up his mind early that as soon as he could save enough money, he would go back to South Carolina. He was making four dollars an hour and trying to save at least fifty dollars a week, not counting the money he sent back to his mother—usually about twenty dollars a week.

So Ernest settled into a routine that seldom varied. He would come home from work, play with Joe Cecil's two children for a while and then watch television until bedtime. Bedtime often was the worst time of the day. At work, he did not have much time to think about his homesickness. But at night, when he could not sleep, he thought a lot about home.

One thing about it, he never did have trouble sleeping at home. When he went to bed at home, he did not have anything to trouble his mind. Nothing to worry about. But in Miami he would lie on his cot and hear the sirens, which seemed to go all night, and he would wonder if somebody had been hurt in a wreck or if somebody had shot somebody else. In Miami everybody was always worried about somebody breaking into their house. But in South Carolina his family never had locked their doors and they never had anybody break in their house or steal anything, and they did not worry about it.

"Just too many people living too close together," he reckoned.

One night, just before the Fourth of July, he was lying on the cot thinking about South Carolina and how pleasant the summer nights are there, and he decided that he had had enough of Miami. He had saved $200—at least he would have that much after the next payday. He could pick up some kind of work at home to hold him until maybe something good would come along.

"I'm going home," he said to himself. "I was born there, and that's all I know and all I like. It's just a way of birth, I reckon. So I'm going home."

The bus brought him back to Kingstree on the Fourth of July.

Chapter Twenty

FORT GREENE

The Brooklyn neighborhood that Donnie Gibson toured briefly that Sunday morning in June is still designated as Fort Greene in the borough president's office and in the offices of the local antipoverty agency. But not many of today's Fort Greene residents know the name of their neighborhood; even fewer of them bother to use it. To most of them the only name known or needed is Brooklyn. The others tend to consider themselves a part of Bedford-Stuyvesant, mainly because the spillover from Bedford-Stuyvesant to Fort Greene in recent years has pretty well wiped out the Classon Avenue dividing line.

A long time ago, maybe four or five decades back, Fort Greene was a proud model of middle-class urban America. Its rows of attached or semi-attached buildings were private homes or comfortable one-family apartments housing doctors and lawyers and businessmen. If the neighborhood could not boast of Manhattan money, neither did it have to contend with the Manhattan crush. Its citizens were the suburbanites of their day, with pretensions and ambitions and family background. Its streets were broad and quiet and its sidewalks were lined with water oaks and elms. Inside the massive brownstones, the look and feel of integrity was reinforced with carpeting and solid mahogany wainscoting.

At first, that is the way Donnie saw the neighborhood —not as it is but as it once was. He was fresh off the farm in a community where indoor plumbing is a measure of affluence and where only the county courthouse and maybe an occasional church building shows the kind of solid permanence of a brownstone, even an old brownstone. Gradually over the next few weeks, he began to see it in a more realistic sense.

Fort Greene in the summer of 1969 was a festering sore of weary brick and brownstone, throbbing with the pus of human despair. Its streets seemed at times to be paved with the flotsam and jetsam of a migrant army— discarded bedsprings; baby carriages; mattresses soaked successively in urine, blood and many rains; broken refrigerators, stoves, washing machines and assorted items of furniture; carcasses of automobiles in various stages of cannibalization. Garbage cans stood battered along the sidewalks, each one presiding over a column of overflow litter running into the streets—milk cartons, crushed aluminum cans, smashed bottles and rotting food scraps.

The surviving trees battled weeds, concrete and garbage for nourishment. Many landlords had given up the battle for economic survival. Rioting in 1964 had been followed by periodic disturbances and steady decay. While upper-story residential rental obviously was booming, ground-level commercial rental had become a bust. One storefront after another stood empty behind broken windows, wooden boards or locked iron bars. Their owners no longer bothered to post FOR RENT signs. Those businesses still operating did their buying and selling in daylight hours, behind display windows prudently and permanently emptied of merchandise.

Fort Greene was a neighborhood where many of the residents seemed to live on the streets—aimlessly, mindlessly wandering from one corner to the next. An old woman could lie sleeping in a public doorway for hours undisturbed, even unnoticed—her legs sprawled on the sidewalk, her body slumped against the door of an empty jewelry store for partial protection against a steady rain. It was a neighborhood constantly assaulting the senses—smell, taste, sight—and the sense of middle-class propriety. Hanging over everything was the pervasive odor of soured garbage, soured wine and soured lives.

Statistically, Fort Greene is about 230 blocks running from Classon Avenue at Atlantic Avenue northwest to the East River. It is home to the Brooklyn Navy Yard, several college campuses and public-housing projects, a great many tenements and more than 100,000 people, one-quarter of whom live on public welfare.

Fort Greene Community Corporation, the local antipoverty organization, has divided the entire section into five areas of roughly equal size. Area One, a forty-two-block square administered from an office only two blocks from Kevin and Renea's apartment on Gates Avenue, is perhaps typical of the entire section. In 1960 its total population was about 35,000, of which fifty-six per cent were black, forty-three per cent white and one per cent "other." A total of 3,627 Puerto Ricans, or 11 per cent, were included as part of the total population figure, but no specific breakdown was given in the 1960 census for Area One. Fifteen per cent of the population had income of less than $2,000 per year, and forty-two per cent were below $4,000. Eight per cent of the population was unemployed. Thirty-five per cent of the housing units were either deteriorated or dilapidated.

In the summer of 1969 Area One had become about seventy per cent black, twenty per cent Puerto Rican and maybe ten per cent white. The neighborhood is described in poverty-program worksheets as one of very poor sanitation and relatively poor housing conditions. "Unemployment was high in 1960, and is undoubtedly higher now; the number of impoverished families has undoubtedly increased; and the percentage of overcrowded and substandard housing units has predictably increased as well. Recent figures from the board of education for local elementary schools reveal that students are averaging from 1.5 to 2 years behind in reading skills."

Fort Greene includes parts of the seventy-ninth, the eightieth and the eighty-eighth police precincts. The seventy-ninth, in the heart of Bedford-Stuyvesant, was once the "busy" precinct—that is, a precinct with a great deal of police activity. But now it has become stabilized as an all-black area and seems to be relatively free of the police problems brought about by neighborhoods in change. Or perhaps the police have simply learned to look the other way. In any case, now it is the remainder of Fort Greene, the eightieth and eighty-eighth precincts, that are the busy ones.

Narcotics and prostitution are the two worst problems. But there is an underlying factor beyond the reach of police, one that makes parts of Fort Greene more of a police problem than any section of Harlem, according to the men who work the precincts. The man in Harlem tends to be more of a permanent resident. If he is not a native New Yorker, he has lived there long enough to become street-savvy. If he does not have a job, he has learned to live adequately by his wits. The man in Fort Greene tends to be a relative newcomer to the city, ill-prepared to survive the pressures of any urban ghetto but especially one like Fort Greene.

"Let's put it this way," a police lieutenant said. "The guy in Harlem is smarter, and he's got more money. Who is likely to be angrier, the guy with a buck in his pocket or the guy who is broke?"

In Fort Greene there is a saying that if you stand on a street corner long enough, you will see somebody you know from South Carolina. Mrs. Mary Fowler, assistant director of the Fort Greene Community Progress Center, knows how true this is, and she also knows what urban life does to some of the youngsters coming up from the South. She can look out her office windows to the corner of Washington and Fulton and see it every day.

"The biggest problem in the neighborhood," she said, "is drugs. And that's the drug headquarters of this area, right out there on the corner. If it was a nice day you couldn't cross the street for the addicts. Some days we have to close up early here because so many of them are hanging around."

And the prostitution "is a shame before God." Drugs, pregnancy and prostitution are prevalent in the schools, she said, and even when the schools are operating, the kids fall behind in their learning. Mrs. Fowler migrated to Brooklyn with her parents when she was three years old. Even as Donnie Gibson and many others like him were arriving in Fort Greene from the South, Mrs. Fowler and many others like her were seriously thinking of leaving the area to return to the South. When schools opened in the fall of 1969, she had decided to send four of her thirteen children South to live with relatives and finish school there.

Fort Greene is a transitional neighborhood in every sense of the word. Among the tens of thousands of uprooted blacks and Puerto Ricans pouring into New York City every year from Southern farms and Caribbean slums, only the weak and weary make Fort Greene their home. For the others it is no more than a waystop, a place where the human spirit survives on dreams of moving back to the South or back to the Caribbean or out to Connecticut.

One of those who looked forward to Connecticut was Sammie Joe Johnson, an easygoing son of the South Carolina soil. Sammie Joe never made it because Fort Greene also is the kind of place where broken dreams are as plentiful as broken furniture.

Sammie Joe finished high school in 1965 and, like his older sister and two older brothers, migrated to Brooklyn confident that a job, good pay and the Good Life waited there for anyone willing to work. He got a job. But somehow the bills always ran ahead of his take-home pay. Back home he had been especially close to his mother, and he was sorely troubled because he could not send her as much money as he wanted to—never as much as the other children sent her. All Sammie Joe really wanted out of life was to be able to send money home to his mother, to marry Joanne—who had come up from Williamsburg County to love him and bear his child—and to move out to Connecticut after they were married.

At Christmas in 1967, he had visited his parents and left in unexplainable tears. One Thursday night the following February, he cried in Joanne's arms.

"Jo," he said. "I'm in pains."

"What kind of pains?" she asked.

"You wouldn't understand," he said.

The next day he had a friend call Joanne and take her to a party as his stand-in. Saturday afternoon he made a rare stop at a bar just off Gates Avenue and ordered a beer, pushing aside an empty can in front of him.

"That's my beer," the man standing beside Sammie Joe said.

"It's empty," Sammie Joe said, offering to buy another.

They exchanged words and then blows, and suddenly a pistol was fired from inside a coat pocket. The bullet passed through the lining of the coat and into Sammie Joe's heart. Sammie Joe made it to the doorway and died there in the arms of two friends who were trying to get him out to the street. "He died in an argument over an empty beer can," Joanne said later. "For no other reason than that."

Donnie Gibson did not know Sammie Joe Johnson, although they had come from the same county in South Carolina. He never met Mrs. Fowler or talked with police in the precinct houses. He only became vaguely aware of the school problems by listening to Kevin and Renea discuss them.

He did not see the neighborhood as it was because there were too many other things to see, too many things to do. That first week in June he covered the streets of Brooklyn for hours on foot and on buses, visiting his brothers and sisters. He learned the subway system by experiment, taking first one train and then another to see where it went. In Manhattan, he knew, he always could find his way home simply by taking the A train of the Eighth Avenue Subway. He went to see the Mets play and to Coney Island. He did not go to Central Park, but he visited Prospect Park, and he found a small field in Fort Greene where a pickup game of sand-lot baseball was to be had almost any day. That little park was to become almost a second home to him as the summer wore on.

He was seldom in the apartment during the first week, and he called home only once, on Thursday. But Kevin and Renea noticed the next week that Donnie was spending a lot of time in the apartment, watching television and halfheartedly playing with the children. He called home three times that week, and Kevin and Renea decided after the third call that it was time for Donnie to go to work. Kevin already had talked with his boss at the retread shop in New Jersey. A job was open on the rubber mold, and Donnie could have it. It was a second-shift job, and it was hot work. But it paid well, and Donnie could ride to work with Kevin. Donnie would have to pay for public transportation only one way, on the return trip at night. They talked about it over the weekend, and Donnie decided to take it. He went to work the next Monday morning, June 16.

On the nineteenth, Donnie called Julia to tell her about the job. Everything was fine, he said. Just fine. He would be making better than a hundred dollars a week.

Renea delivered little Kevin on the twenty-third, and Donnie called Julia again to tell her about it. With the extra baby in the apartment now, he said, he was looking for a place of his own, maybe a room with a kitchenette.

What he did not tell Julia was that life with his older sister was beginning to get a little touchy. It had started, he thought, after his first payday. Renea had certain ideas about what he ought to do with his money, and Donnie had other ideas. She thought he ought to start saving right away. He ought to send some money home. Donnie wanted to buy some clothes first and maybe spend a little on himself. Besides, there was not that much money left after they got through taking out on him. Unless he got overtime he was bringing home only about eighty dollars a week, and it just didn't last long.

After that, things seemed to get worse. Working the rubber mold was the hottest and hardest job in the shop, and Donnie did not like it. Several times he had burned himself. At one point he threatened to quit, but Kevin got him transferred off the mold to another part of the shop. Still, he was not happy with the job. "And if you're not happy on a job," he told himself over and over, "if you don't like what you're doing, then there's no use doing it."

He talked with Geraldine about the situation at the

apartment and found her more understanding. He began spending more and more time at Geraldine's apartment, enjoying the freedom he found there, and gradually began to move his clothes to her apartment.

Worst of all, there was the problem of getting to and from work. Kevin was leaving home earlier now. As a supervisor he reported before the regular shift. Donnie rode with Kevin's brother or one of their friends. If he got a ride to Jersey City, he did not have to leave home until around 2:30 in the afternoon. But often he had to take the subway, which meant taking the subway into Manhattan, changing to the tube for the Jersey side of the river and then taking a bus to the shop. That meant he had to leave home about 2:00. At night he had to repeat the same routine, and he almost never got home until 1:30 or 2:00 in the morning.

He hated the subways and the buses and he hated the second shift, which left him little time to do anything but work and sleep. He met a girl from Alabama who was spending the summer in Brooklyn. He took her to the movies a couple of times, but they did not hit it off and so he did not call her again.

New York, he began to realize, was a hard place to make friends. He just could not understand why everybody was so cold and unfriendly. Down South when you walk along the street and smile to somebody, he smiles back. When you speak to him, he speaks back. In New York if you do that, they look at you like you were crazy. Nobody ever has any time. Everybody is always in a hurry.

By mid-July Donnie knew he did not like New York, anything about it—his job, riding the subways, the people, the whole thing. Yet, when he thought about going back to South Carolina, he knew that that would not work either. Thinking about it, he began to suspect that South Carolina never had been as good a place as it had seemed when he lived there. He wondered now if he had ever really liked it down there. "I don't like it here," he told himself. "But I don't think I like it down there either, so I'll just stay here for a while."

Jersey City seemed like a nice place, and he thought about saving some money and moving over there. But then he knew that would take some time, and he was not all that sure he liked Jersey City. Renea tried to get him to go to a trade school, and Donnie actually called about it. But the school was filled for the fall session, and Donnie was not prepared to make any sort of commitment a year ahead.

There was one way out of his dilemma—join the Navy. He got up early one morning and took a bus to the Navy recruiting office feeling better than he had felt in several weeks. He might just make a career out of the Navy, he thought. Or maybe spend ten or fifteen years in it and then get out and settle down. At the recruiting office, the man asked Donnie if he had registered for the draft yet. Donnie had not. The man allowed as how the chances of getting into the Navy were pretty slim at the time and suggested that Donnie go on and register for the draft first and then check back in several months.

After that, Donnie began to spend more time in the park playing baseball. He also began to find reasons for not going to work. One day he hurt his arm playing ball and could not go in. Several times he missed his ride, or he did not feel well enough to work.

He started a mental game with the telephone. "If Julia calls today with some word on the job applications in South Carolina," he would say to himself, "I'll just go on back home when I get paid on Friday." Julia did not call, and Donnie in his loneliness began to function in a kind of torpor, sleeping later in the mornings, smoking more and trying to think less about his situation. He had found that he could not talk about his problems with his sisters. But late in July, he did have a talk with his brother Archie.

"I don't like it up here either," Archie told him. "I've been thinking about going back South if things don't change."

Donnie agreed to Archie's suggestion that they stick it out until Christmas. If things were not any better by then, they would just pull out together and head home.

Chapter Twenty-one
HOME AGAIN

It was almost the middle of July before the Alstons could make the trip back to North Carolina to pick up their furniture, and Creola wondered for a while if maybe they should not just go on back home to stay.

Washington was fine in a lot of ways. She had been surprised at how well the children took to city life; to tell the truth, she kind of liked it herself. The city had its drawbacks. She could not go to church at night unless she had enough money for a taxi to bring her home, because she was afraid to be on the streets at night. She did not like to leave her children at home very long, even in the daytime, without her or Wash there, especially after that morning she had gone to the store. Martha had left the door unlocked, and a young boy just walked right in the door carrying a bottle of whisky and asked Martha to have a drink with him. Thank God that Martha had had the strength and the good sense to get him out of the house without trouble.

The city was not like home, and Creola did not think that it ever would be. She would never like living there the way she had liked living in Mayflower. But things had not been as unpleasant, for the most part, as she had feared they might be. It was easy to get around once she learned the bus system; most things she needed were convenient. And she had found a church.

Her sister Rosetta had come by for her that first Sunday morning to take Creola to the Evangel Temple on Georgia Avenue. Creola had grave doubts at first because it was not a Baptist church. It was nondenominational. But she went because she did not have another church to go to, and because she felt that Rosetta would choose a good church. When the service was over, Creola was almost surprised to realize that she had enjoyed it. Still, she was not at all sure about joining the church. She would have to think about it.

The thing that really bothered Creola, though, was the house. One thing was sure: she could not go on living in Willie Durham's house.

The trouble had started the first week, when it was time to pay the rent. No, that was not right. It had started even before that—when Willie Durham did not move into the basement the way he said he was going to. Every night, he slept on the sofa in the living room, and most mornings he took his breakfast with the Alstons. He really was living with the Alstons almost as a free boarder, because he also ate supper with them sometimes. But only when it was time to pay the first week's rent did Creola get angry. Wash had told her in North Carolina that the rent would be ninety dollars a month. She had divided that by four and come up with twenty-two dollars and fifty cents a week.

She must have got mixed up, Willie Durham told her. The rent was thirty dollars a week including heat and lights. Creola had been angry almost the whole time since then, although she kept her anger to herself most of the time.

Right after the business about the rent there was a fuss over the draperies. Creola and Martha had worked hard cleaning and scrubbing the living room, trying to make it look like home. They had hung some pictures on the walls, and they had washed the green draperies on the bay window in the living room.

But Willie Durham did not like either the pictures or the way Creola had hung the draperies. She and Martha had hung them loose but bunched up on either side of the window, the way draperies are supposed to be. But Willie Durham thought the draperies ought to be kept closed, even during the day.

"But it's dark in the living room when the draperies are closed," Creola said. "And I don't see any sense in burning a light during the daytime when God has given us his light outside."

Still, Willie Durham wanted the draperies to be kept

closed, and he closed them. Every time he would close them Creola would open them later. Finally, after several days, Willie Durham seemed to give in. He went out and bought some pink ribbon and tied the draperies back with it. If they had to be opened, he said, then he wanted them tied back to stay open.

Creola by this time did not have the energy to continue the fight. But Martha's anger was renewed when she saw Willie Durham's pink ribbons on the green draperies and her mother's almost tearful face. She went into the living room, removed the ribbons from the draperies, and threw them into the garbage.

"Mama, this is ridiculous," she said. "We can't live in this man's house."

That night when Willie Durham came home from work, he saw the draperies without the pink ribbon. "All right," he said. "I'll just take 'em down. Take 'em down." He stored the draperies in the basement. After that the windows remained bare, and Creola knew that she had to move.

She bought a newspaper and began looking at apartments and houses for rent. But she had not found anything suitable when Wash decided the second week in July that they would go get the furniture. That was when Creola thought about going back home to stay. She mentioned it to Wash, and Wash agreed to go back if Creola really wanted to. But Creola knew that Wash did not want to go back, and that the children wanted to stay in Washington. When she had prayed about it for several nights, she knew that she could not think about it again.

They left for North Carolina on Friday, the eleventh.

Wash had not been able to find a truck, so Wiley drove them down in Harvey's car. Wash figured he could rent a trailer in North Carolina if he did not find a truck there.

The land lay green and hot under the blazing July sun—green the way Creola liked it and liked to think of it, but hotter than she remembered. The land was still and perfumed with honeysuckle, summer grain and the clean smell of the pine trees that shaded the lane leading from the paved road down to the Alston place. Creola smelled the earth and felt it, without having to touch it, and she became very sentimental about the land until they got to the house.

The Alston house is a product of the only thing like a construction boom ever to hit the rural South. It is popularly called a "shell" home because that is the name its builders gave it when the house was introduced after the Second World War, and because that was the kind of house the builders set out to build and sell. The basic shell home is little more than a cracker box composed of four walls, a floor and a ceiling. It is considerably less than what middle-class Americans would call an ideal home. It is, in fact, offensive to many of them—an eyesore on the land. But these critics are mostly people who never have been up close to the kind of houses the shell-home buyers leave. For all its lack of elegance, for all its fragility, the shell home offers definite advantages to the small farmers of the Southeast, especially the black farmers. For a few years, at least—until the wood begins to warp from alternate doses of winter dampness and summer heat, until the floors and the walls and the ceiling and the windows begin to groan under the burden of too much wear and too little care—the owner has a roof over his family's head that does not leak. He has walls around him and a floor under him that will take the bite out of the wind and the cold and the dampness. Best of all, he can buy the basic house more easily than he can buy a good car—that is, with less money down and small monthly payments for five to twelve years. If the buyer owns a free title to the land the house is built on, he does not even have to make a down payment, because the builder will take a mortgage on the land as his equity in the house. If he can afford it, or if he is susceptible to salesmanship, the buyer can get more than the basic shell—interior paneling, insulation, even indoor plumbing. He can, by paying more, end up with a house that even middle-class Americans find not too offensive. Among poor black farmers, more often than not, the frills are left to later. That is the plan, at least. And sometimes the pride of home ownership takes hold, and the new home owner really does complete the house later by installing indoor plumbing, adding things he could not afford initially, and even prettying up the place. More often than not, though, the shell-home owner is no more capable of repairing and improving his shell home than he was able to spend money on his old house. The money simply is not available.

Thousands of such homes have been built in the rural South in the past two decades, and the Alston house is one of them. The house has three small bedrooms, a living room and a kitchen. It is partially finished on the inside with wallboard paneling, but it does not have indoor plumbing, and is heated only by a wood-burning stove in the living room.

Outside, the house had changed very little since June, except in the way Creola saw it. When she had left her house it had seemed comfortable enough. She did not mind too much the holes in the screens, the doors that did not close tightly, the stains of red mud. The house then had a lived-in appearance, and besides, it was the best house she had known until she had gone to Washington. Now, she had some basis for comparison, and she knew the difference.

Stopping at Ernest Turner's store on the way home, the Alstons learned that Ernest had not yet found a tenant. But Creola discovered soon after she went inside that somebody had been visiting the house. Somebody had used their bed for fornication and left a discarded symbol of their purpose. As Creola looked at the ugly thing lying there on her bed, she knew she could not sleep in her house that night. She would not be swayed by Wash's reasoning that a change of sheets would remove the thing from her mind. So the boys slept in the house, but Wash and Creola spent the night with Wash's cousin, Emily Stamper, who lives up the road a little ways.

Saturday morning they were up early, for it was to be a busy day. Creola had some things she had to do and some visiting she looked forward to, and she wanted to be back with the children in Washington before dark. They had decided Friday night to rent a trailer to haul as much furniture as they could, and that meant that they would have to drive to Henderson to get it. On the way through Warrenton, Creola stopped and paid all of the $12.41 grocery bill she had left in town, and $15.00 on the furniture bill. It would take a long time to pay off all of the furniture bill, but she would not worry about it as long as she could pay a little something regularly. In Henderson, she visited with her sister while Wash and the boys went to get the trailer. Wash got the biggest one he thought they could afford, but still it was not big enough to carry much. It cost nearly thirty dollars, but ten of that was a deposit they would get back when they turned in the trailer in Washington. At that price, Wash figured he would take the small trailer and then make another trip later to pick up the rest of the furniture.

Even after renting the trailer they still had twenty-five dollars left to pay Ernest Turner on their bill when they stopped for a visit with him and some of the folks at the store. Creola told everybody about Washington, leaving out the bad part about Willie Durham's house, and in return she was given the latest news about the comings and goings of the citizens and former citizens of Mayflower. Georgia Mae Perry had gone North two weeks after graduation. Her family was not sure where she was. Laura Ella Alston, of the Alston family living next to Ernest's store, was getting ready to leave. She had stayed around since graduation hoping for a job, but nothing had come up.

When Ernest told Creola about the plans for the annual Homecoming Revival during the fourth week of August, Creola hesitated before telling Ernest she probably would not be able to come back for it. She really would like to come, she realized. But something had been going around in the back of her mind since they had got back to Mayflower Friday. She was still preoccupied with it later as she supervised the selection of furniture to be loaded on the trailer, settling in the end for two beds without the mattresses and springs, the baby's bed, the television set, two dressers, some dishes and the freezer, which had been Creola's first-priority item.

In the car going back to Washington that Saturday afternoon, Creola had time to think some things out without distraction, and so she returned to what had been nagging at her. In this business about where their home was going to be, Creola knew that it was time for her to take stock of herself and see what she was doing and what she was supposed to be doing—what ought to be done and what ought not to be done.

The way it looked to her now, her family wanted to live in Washington instead of North Carolina. Well, if that was the case, then she had to make up her own mind about some things. First, she had to stop thinking of North Carolina as home. She had to put North Carolina behind her and start thinking of Washington as her home. They would have to come back one more time for furniture, and they could come back now and then to visit—although Creola could not help wondering how many people would be left to visit in a few years. But the important thing was to get it straight in her heart and in her head just where her home was going to be. To Creola's way of thinking, it did not matter too much what her own preference might be. What counted was the way her family felt about it. Still, when she did examine her own feelings, she found a surprising agreement with her family. One thing kept coming back to her repeatedly. She could admit something to herself now that she had tried not to admit when they were living in North Carolina. Wash's drinking had become more of a problem than she had ever let on. It had got to the point in the last year or so where Wash actually seemed to look forward to nothing more than the weekend, when he could buy a quart or a half-gallon of liquor on Friday night and stay drunk until Monday morning. Since they had moved to Washington, though, a change had come over Wash, and she found it hard to believe that it had happened in so short a time. Wash did not seem to need liquor the way he had in North Carolina. He still drank. But he did not get drunk any more. Although now and then he would buy a half-pint of whisky, usually it was only a carton of beer on paydays, and that would last him all week.

By the time they got into Washington that evening, Creola had worked out her thoughts and made some decisions. Until the Lord shows me otherwise, she decided, Washington is going to be our home. And if Washington is going to be our home, then I am going to find a decent house for us to live in. If we can't manage it on what we're making now, then I'll go to work.

Chapter Twenty-two

GEORGIA MAE TAKES A RIDE

When the last month of school began, Georgia Mae Perry's family still thought she would move to Washington and stay with her sister, Patricia. Patricia was coming home for the graduation, and Georgia Mae was supposed to go back to Washington with her. But Georgia Mae went to Washington the second weekend in May to visit Patricia, and she knew then that she had to eliminate another choice.

The visit had gone all right until Sunday afternoon, when Georgia Mae was getting ready to go back home. It was Patricia who mentioned it first. "When you come up here to stay," she said, "it's gonna be another second home for you. I'll be just like Mama was."

At first Georgia Mae thought she was kidding.

"No. I mean it," Patricia said. "It's gonna be just like home. I'm gonna be just as strict with you and just as tight on you as Mama was."

The two of them were sitting in the living room of Patricia's apartment, and Georgia Mae sat and looked at her sister for a long time before she answered.

"Pat, why do you think I'm leaving home?"

"I don't know," Patricia said. "But I know what you're gonna do when you get here."

So that was that. Someplace else she could not go,

Georgia Mae thought. Pat was only six years older than Georgia Mae. Pat had been at the house in Warrenton that night in February. If Pat did not understand, then Georgia Mae could not expect anybody in the family to understand. If she could not move in with Pat after graduation, then she might as well cut loose from the family completely. Georgia Mae did not know whether she was angry or just hurt inside as she left Patricia's apartment.

"When you come home for my graduation," she said to Patricia, "then I'll let all of you know where I'm going—and it won't be Washington. I'm not coming to Washington, and I'm not going to stay with any of my people. I don't want to go nowhere where I'm not welcome or where there's always gonna be some back talk."

There never had been any question about whether Georgia Mae would stay in Warrenton or leave when she was through high school. She knew she could support herself in Warrenton. She could support herself anywhere because she could type, and she could sew well enough to make a living at it. She had made almost enough money sewing for people to pay for her sewing machine and most of her own clothes for the past two years. She had made everything she wore except three dresses, and she wished each time after she bought one of them that she had not bought it, because she could have made it better for less money. Counting her sewing, her salary from the church, her pay for working in the school office in the Neighborhood Youth Corps and the money she made from driving the school bus, she had averaged from $125 to $150 a month all through the senior year. If she could do that well while she was going to school, she knew she could support herself after graduation.

But Georgia Mae never had planned to stay in Warrenton after high school—not since she was old enough to think for herself, at least, and certainly not for the past two years. There might have been a time before that when she thought about getting a job and living in Warrenton. She could not remember it, though. If she ever had considered it, she could not stay in Warrenton now. Too much had happened in two years. Too many things had changed. In two years her whole life had changed. She knew lots of people said that when they were about to graduate from high school. But in her case it was true, and she wished it wasn't so.

It seemed to Georgia Mae that things had got worse gradually. Her mother was sick a lot during the senior year, and Georgia Mae had met Frank. Her mother did not like her dating Frank, as usual. Her mother did not like her to have any boyfriends at all, it seemed to Georgia Mae. But she kept on dating Frank anyway.

Georgia Mae Perry was not the prettiest girl in school. But she was not bad looking either. Her skin was jet black, and her facial features were thick and sharp, almost Caucasian. She had long hair, and she spent a lot of time keeping it looking neat. Except for her size, she would have been beautiful. She was not fat, although she was overweight. She was just big—tall and broad-shouldered, thick through the chest and hips and arms and legs.

Georgia Mae had had her first love affair when she was fifteen. The boy was two years older than she was, and she had dated him for two years, until he graduated and went to New York. After that, Georgia Mae did not go out much with boys until she met Frank Baskett. One reason was that not many tall boys were available. But mostly it was just to keep down trouble at home. Besides, she was pretty busy with her jobs and with trying to keep up her grades.

When she met Frank, she knew he was different from other boys she had dated. Her mother did not like it, of course, and Georgia Mae asked her mother once why she made such a fuss about Georgia Mae's going out with boys.

"We've got one mistake in the family," her mother said, "and I don't want to have another one."

Georgia Mae knew she was talking about Patricia. Pat had got pregnant before she was married, and the man she married was not the father of the child. Georgia Mae's mother had taken the baby, and was raising him now as her own. Norman and Eugene had had some trouble in their marriages, too. Both of them lived at home now, and their wives lived up North.

"But Mama," Georgia Mae said, "you can't judge one person by another, because no two people are alike. Just because it happened once, there's no reason to think it will happen to me."

Her mother would not talk about it. "My mama was strict on me," she said, "and I'm gonna be strict on you."

The way Georgia Mae and Aaron saw it, their mother just did not want them to associate with anybody at all. Thirteen-year-old Aaron, the youngest of the six children and the one Georgia Mae felt closest to, was beginning to feel the pressure, too.

The relationship between Georgia Mae and her mother got steadily worse during the senior year. Her mother not only disapproved of Frank and the amount of time Georgia Mae was spending with him; she also began to show a concern for Georgia Mae's financial affairs. Her mother could not understand what Georgia Mae was doing with her money, and thought she ought to be contributing more to the cost of running the household.

For a long time, Georgia Mae simply did not answer when her mother asked her about her money. But then one day in January, after her mother had talked especially sharply about it, Georgia Mae figured she had had enough. She called the furniture store in town and asked them to deliver the furniture she had been paying for secretly on lay-away. Her mother couldn't get over it when the truck came out with a sofa, two living-room chairs, two end tables, a coffee table, three rugs and a kitchen cabinet.

All her mother could say was, "You shouldn't have done it" and "Why didn't you tell me?" and "Why did you do it?" Georgia Mae knew why, but she could not tell her mother. She wanted to have something of her own. She wanted to have a nice home, a place she could be proud of and could bring her friends to.

With the new furniture, the house looked real nice, Georgia Mae thought. She and her brothers already had added a room onto the back of the house, to make five rooms altogether, and she had added an indoor bath. After the furniture came, Georgia Mae put up some wallpaper herself. The place really looked nice. It looked like home.

The new furniture brought a temporary peace between Georgia Mae and her mother in their quarrels about money. But the other problem—the constant fuss about what Georgia Mae did with her own time—did not improve at all. In fact, Georgia Mae could feel it getting worse, and she wondered if she could put up with it until school was out. They really had a big fuss around the end of January, when Georgia Mae came home from a basketball game. Her mother had said she couldn't go, but Georgia Mae went anyway. She had reached the point where she just tried to ignore her mother.

Georgia Mae went on living in her mother's house. There was no place else for her to go. She and her mother hardly talked to one another at all. Georgia Mae spent as little time at home as she could get by with, and her mother did not argue with her any more when she went out. Except when she was with Frank, Georgia Mae did not really live. She existed, functioning almost mechanically. She did not go out much, not even with Frank, because she had to work as much as she could and save as much money as she could. She failed one of her courses and had to settle for a certificate at graduation instead of a diploma. The thing she thought about most was where she would go when school was out. After the visit with Pat she knew she could not live with her. She certainly was not going to stay at home.

Frank wanted her to go to New York after graduation. She could live with his parents until she found a place. But Georgia Mae was not sure that was what she wanted, either. She simply could not make a decision.

Frank left the day after graduation, and Georgia Mae still had not told him whether she would come to New York. All she could say was maybe. She had to wait a week because she had to turn in the bus and then wait for her final paycheck to come by mail from the school board.

The second week after graduation some of her friends offered her a ride to Washington in their car. She accepted because she could get that far and save money on travel expenses. When she got there, she would decide then what to do, where to go.

At the end of the summer, Georgia Mae's family still did not know where she was. They had heard from one of Georgia Mae's aunts, who was living in Washington. Georgia Mae had stayed there for a while, but then she had found a job in Baltimore, the aunt thought.

All anyone could say with any certainty was that Georgia Mae was up North.

Chapter Twenty-three

A MATTER OF PRIDE

Wash and Rosetta did not want Creola to go to work when she told them, the Sunday after they got back from North Carolina, about what she planned to do. They were worried about her health. Creola had lost about ten pounds since they had moved. But she knew that was nothing in the world except worry about the house. She knew her own strength. She knew it better than they did, and she knew she could not sit around the house just wringing her hands and worrying about a place to live.

Monday morning, when she had got Wash off to work and finished her housework, Creola put on a good dress and told Martha to look after the other children. She had a little more than ten dollars in her bag, and she knew that would buy at least a small ad in the newspaper. She rode the bus downtown and went into the advertising department at the Washington *Post*. The woman at the counter helped Creola write out a short classified ad saying that Creola wanted a job as a domestic. Creola paid $5.40 to have the ad run three days, and she went back home feeling better than she had felt in weeks.

The ad brought better results than Creola had expected. People even came by her house instead of waiting to write. Creola had more job offers than she could take, so she made up her mind according to how well she liked the people. She already had decided that she would work only three days a week. She would not work on Friday, Wash's day off, and she felt that working all week would keep her away from too many duties at home. The way it worked out, she took two jobs. On Tuesdays and Wednesdays she worked for a Mrs. Stafford, who worked at a radio station, and on Saturdays she worked for Mrs. Richard McCarthy, whose husband was a congressman. Both homes were in Maryland, and Creola had to ride three different buses to get to the McCarthy home and two different buses to the Stafford home. But Creola did not mind. She soon found that she really did enjoy working for the two families because everybody was so nice and pleasant.

Each job paid twelve dollars a day plus bus fare, and Creola was determined that the extra thirty-six dollars a week would go toward better housing. Most days when she was not working, she was looking at apartments and houses. She never would have thought housing would be so hard to find in a city with so many buildings. But day after day, week after week, her search for a decent place to live went the same way. The place was too small for her large family, or cost more money than they could afford, or was in a bad neighborhood. Creola was determined that one thing had to be right. She had to be satisfied that her family would be living in a good neighborhood.

Once she found a ten-room house off Park Road that seemed perfect. But on the street outside the house, she saw three little boys no bigger than her George and Robert shooting craps right there on the sidewalk, and nobody paid any attention. Older people just stood around watching or walked right by without saying anything to the youngsters. She would not allow her children to live in a neighborhood like that.

The situation at Willie Durham's house was growing worse, too. Creola was so happy to have her freezer when they got back from North Carolina that she plugged it up the day they got back. She figured she would give it a few days to get cold, and then maybe she could start putting some things in it.

But the very next day, Sunday morning, she came down to the kitchen to start breakfast, and she noticed that the freezer was unplugged. She did not understand how it had come unplugged, but she plugged it back.

Willie Durham came downstairs after Wash left for work. He saw that the freezer was plugged into the wall socket, and right away he walked over without a word and unplugged it.

Then Willie turned to Creola and said, "You ain't got nothing in that freezer except water. I just wish you wouldn't run it."

Creola could not control her anger at the man any more.

"Mr. Durham," she said, "let me tell you one thing. I pay you rent, and if I don't have nothing in there it's not any of your concern. You're getting your rent, and as long as we pay our rent that's it. As long as you get your money you don't have anything to say about our freezer."

It was the first time that Creola really had talked back to Willie that strongly, and Willie was so taken aback he could not answer.

"Wait a minute," he said. "Now wait a minute."

"Wait a minute, nothing. I mean what I say."

Willie Durham stormed out of his house and got in his car and drove all the way to Arlington to complain to Wash, the way he always did when he and Creola had a spat of some kind. Wash was a little upset when he came home that evening. He was tired of hearing Willie Durham's complaints. But he knew there was not much they could do except try to keep the peace as long as they lived in Willie's house.

"Honey," he told Creola, "just unplug the freezer. We don't want that kind of confusion."

"Well, to my way of thinking, it ain't confusion at all," Creola said. "I was just standing up for my right, and he was just being natural-born mean."

Creola kept the freezer plugged in and asked forgiveness in her prayers that night. She felt almost sick about the whole thing.

There was no more trouble about the freezer. But the refrigerator became a problem after that. Willie Durham kept some of his own food in the refrigerator, and sometimes he would have a friend over to eat with him. But he did not keep his things in a separate place in the refrigerator. He just put them in anywhere, mixing them with the Alstons' food. The children never did know what was theirs and what was Willie Durham's, and sometimes they would eat food that belonged to Willie. That caused constant arguments.

Then the oven in the stove had not worked since the Alstons moved in, and Creola felt bad about going next door every few days to bake bread in the neighbor's oven. Every time she mentioned the oven to Willie Durham it caused another argument. Finally, one Saturday near the end of July, Creola had taken all of it she could take. She and Willie Durham almost came to blows—when she thought about it later, she could not even remember what caused the argument—and Creola ordered Willie Durham out of the house.

"Just pack your clothes right now and get out," she told him. "It might be your house, but it's ours as long as we pay you the rent."

Willie Durham packed all his clothes into his station wagon and left the car parked on the street. The next night somebody stole Willie's clothes out of the car, and

Creola felt awfully bad. She had to pray real hard when she got home from church that night. "Dear Lord, forgive me. I don't regret what I told him but I do regret the way I told him. I told him in anger, and I know that is not Christlike. . . ." She wondered and hoped that it was not her fault that Willie's clothes had been stolen.

Willie Durham gave up two weeks later. He sold the house to Mr. Douglas, the man living on the third floor. But Creola was not at all sure things would be any better with the new owner, and she was right. Mr. Douglas made it plain right off that he did not want the Alstons as renters. When he put down roach killer, it was only in his apartment upstairs, which meant that the roaches got worse downstairs. Creola put out rat poison herself after the children saw a rat in the back yard that was as big as a puppy. When the nights began to turn chilly, Mr. Douglas decided himself when the heat would be turned on and off. He complained constantly about how noisy the children were. Finally, it got to the point where Creola knew what Mr. Douglas was going to say every time she paid him the weekly rent—that he wanted them out of the house as soon as they could find something else.

Creola had hoped to have another place to live before the children started school, but it did not work out that way. With her large family, it was just impossible to find a house big enough that they could afford.

She saved all the money she earned from her two jobs plus some from Wash's salary, and at one point in the summer, she had nearly $200. She decided she would try to buy a house, and she found one with three bedrooms and a basement that she really liked. The boys could sleep in the basement because it was heated. But the real-estate man told her a few days later that they could not qualify for the loan.

When school started, there was no one left to look after the babies, and Creola gave up her Tuesday and Wednesday job with Mrs. McCarthy and did most of her house hunting on Wash's day off and some afternoons after the older children came home from school. Although she kept the Saturday job, the loss of income hurt because it came at a time when the family expenses increased. The children needed clothes and lunch money, and the taxis cost a lot of money. Creola had made a habit of taking a taxi to look at a house and then riding the buses back. She did not have much time to look on each trip, and the one-way taxi saved her a lot of time because she could just tell the driver the address instead of having to figure out a bus schedule.

When one of her neighbors suggested in September that Creola apply for food stamps, she thought it over and decided that it was a good idea. Buying food stamps, after all, was not exactly like taking welfare, and they did help a lot on the food bill. Twice a month, she bought eighty-one dollars' worth of stamps for fifty-five dollars in cash. She also signed up for Medicaid, at her neighbor's suggestion. Maybe when she had time and had all the other things behind her, Creola thought, she could get some new teeth with Medicaid.

By the middle of October, the $200 in savings was almost gone, and Creola still had not found a house. On Thursday, a day early, she went upstairs to pay the weekly rent, and Mr. Douglas refused to accept it. "You keep your money and find a place to move," he said. "I'm disgusted and I want you out of the house." If they were not out pretty soon, he added, he would get papers to have them evicted.

Again, Wash and Creola considered moving back to North Carolina. But this time it was Wash who suggested it, and Creola who decided against it. Washington was their home now, and they were going to stay and make it a good home. The kids were happier in school now than they had ever been. If they went back to North Carolina they would have to go further in debt to fix up the house, and they would have to pay somebody to move them back. Creola had learned to like the city—or certain things about it. In Washington, the children did not have to leave for school until 8:30. In North Carolina, some of them had to leave at 7:00 and others at 7:30 to catch the buses, which sometimes they missed. They often had to stand in the rain and cold for half an hour waiting for a bus. In Washington, they could walk to school almost in the time it took them to walk to the paved road in North Carolina.

As important as anything else, Creola had found a church that she liked even better than Saint Stephen. She had come to like Evangel Temple so well that she had been baptized there in late summer. It was not that she liked Saint Stephen any less, and certainly she could never say anything bad about it. But it was just that she liked Evangel Temple better. The pastor at Saint Stephen did not have the learning and the education that Brother Mears and the assistant pastor, Brother Larson, did. The sermons were different. The singing and praying were different, too. At Saint Stephen, the choir

A Matter of Pride

did most of the singing. The congregation sang some, too. But at Evangel Temple, everybody sang together and prayed together. Even when the pastor was praying, everybody in the audience was invited to help him. She could not put down her old church. But then she just could not say enough good about her new church, either, and she was not going to leave it. Wash had even told her, just after she was baptized, that he wanted to go to church with her sometime when he was not working Sundays any more.

No. They were not going to move back to North Carolina. These were dark days now, but surely God would show them some light soon. The light did not come before another day of darkness.

Creola asked for help every night in her prayers and again in church the following Sunday, and still she did not feel that her prayers were being heard. Instead of staying around for a while to chat with Rosetta and some of her new friends at the church, as she normally did, Creola excused herself right after the service was over. She just had to go home and do some more thinking and praying, she told Rosetta.

Mr. Douglas was waiting downstairs when Creola got home, ready to complain about the noise the children had been making. Creola took the complaint almost without thinking about it and worried all afternoon, sending up several of her little prayers.

Toward suppertime, Mr. Douglas came down to the second floor to complain again. One thing that bothered Mr. Douglas especially was when water was left running, and one of the girls had left the water running in the bathroom. Mr. Douglas heard it and came down the stairs, opened the bathroom door and went right into the Alston bathroom without bothering to see if anybody was inside. That made Creola really angry, and for a minute or so she was snapped out of her worrying mood.

"If the water is running," she told Mr. Douglas, "then it's your place to come to me and tell me it's running and ask me to cut it off. I've got two teen-age girls, and it's not your place to barge right into our bathroom like that without checking to see whether somebody is in it."

What Mr. Douglas needed, Creola suggested to him, was a talk with God.

"Don't you talk to me about God," Mr. Douglas said, and he went back to the third floor.

Creola wondered what kind of man would say a thing like that. When Wash came home, Creola told him what had happened and asked him to go upstairs and talk to Mr. Douglas. Creola followed Wash part of the way up the stairs and stood listening to the conversation. When she heard Wash start cussing, she knew that things were not going well. Wash never cussed except when he was mad.

"Just come on down, Wash. He knows everything, and you can't talk to him. You can't tell him anything," Creola said.

That night Creola prayed it out, and she knew later that her prayers had been heard. "Dear Lord, you know our troubles. Lord, show me the way. Show me the light. Guide me. Tell me what to do. . . ."

Creola slept peacefully that night, knowing what she had to do. The next morning when she had got Wash off to work and the older children to school and Michael and Emily in Head Start and kindergarten, Creola dressed little Hosea in warm clothes and took the bus downtown.

In all the time they had lived in North Carolina, the Alstons had never applied for welfare, even in the worst times, and it was a matter of pride with Creola that they had not. But pride was one thing, and her family's well-being was another thing. She would swallow her pride. At the very least, the welfare might help her find a house.

Chapter Twenty-four

THE CROP AND THE DRAFT

Almost any man, if he has a strong back, can find work in the harvest season throughout tobacco country. It is not good work or permanent work. But it is work.

The crop must be harvested, and that is day labor that does not last very long. But when the crop is harvested and sold on the warehouse floors, there is more work available—maybe two or three or four months for the strong or the lucky. From the sales warehouses, the tobacco is transferred to a packing plant nearby, where it is stuffed into huge wooden barrels called hogsheads for shipment to the buyers' processing plants. The packing plants operate only for several weeks after the close of harvest. But it is sometimes possible to find additional work at a processing plant, if one is located near enough, for they often operate until December or January.

Amos and Ernest went to work in one of the packing plants in Kingstree when it opened July 23. They did not really want to work in the plant; the work was hard and the pay was not good. But there was nothing else available. The packing plant would be open for about six weeks, and they figured they could save enough money during that time to pay for a bus ticket. Or maybe they would find a job around home by then. Both of them had made the rounds the week after they got home, applying at the Georgia Pacific plant in Russellville and the wool plant at Jamestown. Amos also had applied for a job with a construction company that was building an addition to the Baxter Laboratories plant. They waited two weeks, not doing much of anything, and then the third week they went to work.

The packing plant in July and August was like a hot oven, except that the air inside an oven would have been cleaner. The tobacco was dumped at one end of the building in loosely tied burlap sheets. It had to be packed into the barrels by hand, and then the barrels had to be put under a hydraulic press that packed the tobacco tight. When that was done, the barrel cover was pressed on, and then the barrels had to be stored at the opposite end of the building to be loaded onto the trucks. The air inside the building was thick with flying tobacco dust that never seemed to settle.

Amos and Ernest had probably the easiest jobs available in the small plant, if any could be called easy. Ernest operated the press and Amos ran the fork-lift that took the barrels out of the press and moved them to the shipping door. They stripped to the waist before going in to work each morning, partly for coolness and partly to save their shirts, although they were not sure that it was any cooler.

The work held up well for the first month. They were making $1.65 an hour, and each of them cleared a total of $180 for the month. After that the work fell off, and by Labor Day they were out of work again.

Driving around town one Saturday night in August, the three of them—Amos and Ernest and James McClary—decided they would leave Kingstree the week after Labor Day. It would be great, they agreed, if they could stick together. Trouble was, they couldn't agree on where to go. James definitely was going to Rochester. He had already made contact with Willie Chandler, and Willie told him he could stay at his place with Willie's cousin. Amos said he would like to go back to Rochester. Only thing was, he did not think his mother would be too happy about that, now that he did not have any relatives living up there.

"You know how old folks are," he said. "Sometimes you gotta go along with them." He thought he might go to Florida to stay with his brother or maybe his aunt.

Ernest definitely was not going back to Florida. He was not at all sure he wanted to go to Rochester, no matter what Amos said about it. He had heard a lot of good things about Florida, too, and look how that turned out.

As it worked out, Ernest was not able to go with either one of the others. He was a year older than they were, and had registered for the draft in the summer of 1968. The last week in August, he got his notice to report for the examination. He had to go to Columbia on September 15 for the examination, and that meant he could not leave until after that.

Amos left for Fort Lauderdale the Tuesday after the Labor Day weekend. His mother had talked with Amos's aunt, who lived in Fort Lauderdale, and she said there were good jobs available in construction work. James McClary left for Rochester the following Tuesday. Ernest was the only one left of the Fantastic Four.

On the fifteenth, Ernest went to Columbia for the draft tests. When he and a bunch of others had finished the written part, they were sent into another room and waited for about half an hour. Then a sergeant came in and started calling off the names of some of the others. He gave the papers back to them. Ernest's name was not called, and one of the soldiers told him, "Buddy, that means you're suitable for Army duty."

Ernest was almost glad. That solved a lot of problems and saved him from having to think and worry too much about what he was going to do.

On the seventeenth, Ernest left by bus for Rochester. He was not especially looking forward to it, but he had never been there and it couldn't be any worse than Florida. At least he could work for a while and maybe put away a little money. Rochester was as good a place as any to wait for the draft, he reckoned.

Chapter Twenty-five

HOME IS NOT HOME ANY MORE

Otis and Julia were sitting on the porch the Tuesday after Donnie left home when Roosevelt McClary came by to give Donnie his graduation present.

Otis was just finishing his dinner on the tray in front of him, and Julia was stringing a bucketful of snap beans to be canned later.

"Hey," McClary called, as he got out of the car and started walking across the freshly swept yard. "You folks doin' all right today?"

"Oh, pretty good, I reckon," Julia said. "You getting along?"

"Fair. Heat's about to get me down though."

McClary laid his hat down on the edge of the porch and wiped a handkerchief across his forehead and then down each cheek and around his neck at the collar line.

"Donnie home today?" he asked.

"No," Julia said. "Donnie done gone."

"Gone? Where'd he go?"

"Gone to New York. Left Saturday."

"I'll be doggone. Left already, huh?" McClary said. "Coming back, though, ain't he?"

"Well, he said he might stay and he might come back," Julia said. "But I ain't looking for Donnie to stay. He likes it too much down here."

"Nah," McClary said. "Donnie ain't gonna stay. He'll be back. Donnie ain't gonna like it up there at all."

They chatted a while longer, and then McClary reached into his hip pocket and pulled some money out of his wallet.

"You give this to Donnie," he said to Julia, handing her two one-dollar bills. "Tell him I'm sorry I didn't get by sooner. But I just didn't have no idea Donnie'd be leaving."

Julia thanked him. She knew Donnie would appreciate it, she said. She would give his regards to Donnie the next time he called.

McClary replaced his hat and started back toward the car, shaking his head. "How 'bout that," he said. "Left already. But he won't stay."

"No," Julia said, bending again to her beans. "I really ain't looking for Donnie to stay. Up there ain't like down here."

Otis asked every day whether Julia thought Donnie would call that day. Every time the telephone rang, he wondered if it was Donnie. By the time they had got the first call that Sunday morning, Otis had asked Julia at least three times to call New York to see if he had got there yet.

Everyone in the Gibson family can read and write. But it is not a writing family. The older boys had written some when they were in the service, but since then the Gibsons had stayed in touch with one another by telephone. Thus, Otis and Julia got no letters from Donnie. They had no words to study and analyze for hidden feelings. The only means they had of gauging

Donnie's well-being throughout that summer was the sound of his voice and the frequency of his calls.

The first week he was gone, Julia thought she could feel the excitement in his voice when he called. It was maybe like the time when Otis brought home the bicycle, or when Donnie got his first baseball glove. The second week, it was different. Julia knew without any doubt that Donnie was homesick. After that, it was hard to tell. Donnie did not call as often, and when he called or when she called New York, it was hard to find out anything about him. She began to feel that he was drifting away from them.

Then one hot afternoon in the middle of August, just as Julia was taking Otis's lunch tray back into the house, Donnie called. He was at the bus station in Kingstree and needed a ride home. Jessie drove to Kingstree and picked him up.

Julia did not ask Donnie whether he planned to stay home. She was happy enough to have him back, and she understood without asking that he would stay if he could find a job. Donnie did not volunteer anything definite. On the contrary, he deliberately tried to create the impression that he was just back for maybe a week or so. It was a means of salvaging some of his pride, or erasing part of the feeling of guilt and defeat, which he could not define clearly. Others in the family were aware of a definite change in the old family relationship, and there was present an element of tension, of uneasy politeness, within hours after the initial family reunion. Even the relationship between Donnie and Otis had changed. Once when Otis wanted to be lifted out of his wheelchair to hitch up his trousers, it was Jessie he asked to lift him, although Donnie was sitting on the porch with Jessie and Otis.

Donnie had been struck by change when Jessie turned into the sandy lane to the house that afternoon. Coming through North Carolina on the bus he had felt a kind of familiar warmth as he watched the fields zip past the bus window. The corn was green, and the tobacco stalks were heavy and full with leaves. As Jessie's car passed the cornfield in front of the Gibson farm, though, Donnie was shocked to see that the corn was brown already. The tobacco stalks had been stripped clean by a harvest that was gone, the first one he had ever missed. Cotton already was beginning to peep through the bolls in the little patch in front of the house.

The place, which never had been much of a farm anyway, was not a farm at all any more. Gray, the old mule that had been a part of the family for as long as Donnie could remember, had been sold in July. A man in Kingstree paid Julia fifty dollars for him. Julia also had sold the two hogs. A few chickens pecking around the backyard were the only stock left.

The most startling thing about the place was the weeds. Donnie never had seen the weeds as high around the yard as they were the afternoon when Jessie drove him home from the bus station. He wondered again if he had done the right thing.

But now he was back with maybe seventy-five or eighty dollars to show for the summer's work, no prospects of a job any time soon, and home was not like home any more.

In bed that night, he asked himself if he had made a mistake in going to New York. No, he decided. "If I'd stayed here," he said to himself, "I wouldn't have been satisfied till I went to see if New York was like they said it was. But what am I going to do now? I don't want to go back to New York, and I don't want to stay down here, and I don't know where to go next."

Briefly, he thought about praying. He had not prayed since that time on the train to New York. But he decided he was too tired, too mixed up, to pray.

The next morning, he got the lawn mower out, went to the store to get a gallon jar of gasoline, and started mowing the weeds and grass around the house.

"Maybe they just look higher than they've ever been because I wasn't here to watch them grow," he told himself as he pushed the mower through the weeds.

He would try the Navy again, he thought. Or maybe the Marines. "I'll do it pretty soon," he said to himself, "sometime soon."

Chapter Twenty-six

THANKSGIVING

The Alstons did not qualify for welfare—not for financial help. But Creola did get some advice from the social worker she talked with. One thing the social worker told her was not to worry too much about being forced to move. She should be a good tenant. She should offer to pay the rent every week and make sure she always had on hand the total amount of rent due at any time. And she should keep looking for another place to live. On that basis the Alstons stayed at Mr. Douglas's house for almost another month.

Then, on a Thursday in November, the week before Thanksgiving, Creola saw an ad about a house for rent on Ninth Street. It had three bedrooms, and the rent was $130 a month. She called the real-estate man, and he told her to go on out to the house because a key was in the mailbox.

When Creola got to the house, it was locked and there was no key in the mailbox. She called the real-estate man again, and he told her to come to the office and pick up a key. Creola already had paid $1.10 for a taxi, but she figured it would be worth another taxi ride because the house did look pretty good on the outside. At the real-estate office, the man looked for the key and could not find it.

"I'm awfully sorry," he said. "But if you will come back tomorrow we'll have a key by ten o'clock." Creola could not hold back her disappointment. She already had spent $2.20 on taxi fares, and now she would have to make the trip again. "Tell you what," the man said. "I've got another house you might want to look at. It has four bedrooms, and I know there's a key in the mailbox there." The house was on Twelfth Street, close to schools and everything, and Creola thought it sounded good—even though the rent was higher. "Here's the address," the man said, writing it on a piece of paper. "You go on out, and if you like it you call me back."

When Creola saw the house at 1611 Twelfth Street, N.W., the thought struck her again that the Lord works in mysterious ways. She liked the house from the outside. It was built too close to the street, but there was a sidewalk and a little iron fence around the front yard.

Inside, Creola saw that the house needed some fixing up. But it looked sound. It had a living room, dining room, spare room and kitchen downstairs, and four bedrooms upstairs. At the back was a yard and a cement porch.

Creola was talking to herself as she went through the house, and talking to her God. "The place is not beautiful," she said to herself, "but it's a blessing from God. The thing is we can make it beautiful." And to her God, Creola said, "Lord, thank you. I know you have guided me to the right place. I know it's better than where I'm at, and I thank you."

When she took Wash by to see it the next day, he liked it, too, and she was glad. It all needed painting badly, and the doors kind of sagged in some places. "But we're not gonna use that as an excuse," Wash said, "because even I can fix doors." Creola knew God had had a hand in it when they got back home that afternoon. There was an eviction notice in the mail. They were supposed to appear before a U.S. marshal the following Monday.

"Thank God, that's one meeting we won't have to go to," Creola thought.

Harvey found a man with a truck who agreed to move the family for thirty dollars, and they started moving out early Saturday morning. Wash had to go to work, but he had called the man at the motel and arranged to get off early to help finish the moving.

Before Willie Durham sold the house, the Alstons had bought some of his furniture. Creola paid him $45 for the dining-room table and chairs, the living-room rug, some tables and all the beds, and she had insisted on a receipt from him. It said that the Alstons actually owned all the furniture in the house, but Creola did not want some of it. Mainly, she was interested in the dining-room set, the rug and the beds.

The moving went smoothly during the first truckload from downstairs. But when they started loading the truck again with the things from the second floor, Mr. Douglas came down to watch.

Creola had packed some boxes that were sitting on one of the beds they had bought from Willie Durham. She sent the boxes down, and then she and Gary started taking down the bed.

"No, no. You can't take that bed," Mr. Douglas said. "You cannot have that bed."

"I most certainly can, and I'm going to," Creola said. "I've got a receipt saying I can take it."

They were still arguing over the bed when Harvey came back upstairs, and Creola saw that Harvey was angry. Suddenly she was scared. Harvey was so angry that she was afraid he might do something to start trouble.

Creola tried to calm everybody to stop a fight, and then she ran downstairs and next door to her neighbor's telephone and called the police. They got the bed out and all the other furniture while the police were there, and there was no further trouble. Creola had forgot the bed in the basement, one she also had bought from Willie Durham, until the police had gone. But she decided to leave it. It would not be worth the trouble that might start again.

With the furniture out of the house, she was rid of Mr. Douglas and Willie Durham and the house and all the trouble they had had there since they moved to Washington six months ago. They had a house of their own now, and Creola knew that things would be better. That night, the first night in their own home, Creola prayed. She prayed and planned and dreamed, and was as full of joy as she had been in a long time.

The house was dirty and kind of run down, and it would take a lot of cleaning and painting and work to get it livable; but still, it was so wonderful to think that she and her family had their own place now, a place where nobody could come in and say this or say that.

The house would be more expensive; the rent was $139 a month, and that did not include heat and lights. That would add another fifty or sixty dollars a month, the best Creola could figure it.

Tuesday, when Wash got paid, Creola bought some turkey parts to cook for Thanksgiving dinner. But that night, Harvey came by with a fourteen-pound turkey and a bagful of cranberries, dressing and some sweet potatoes.

"Mama," he said, "it's been a long time since I had one of your sweet-potato pies. Will you make one for Thanksgiving?"

Creola cooked and cried for joy and praised God. "We'll make it," she said to herself over and over. "Somehow, thank God, we'll make it."

EPILOGUE

The Alstons did make it. It was not easy for them, and it is still tenuous. But they think of themselves now as residents of Washington.

When I visited with them one Saturday in October of 1970, Creola was wearing a new dress, and she looked almost radiant—healthier and more beautiful than I had ever seen her. The thing that made her happiest was that her family was whole again. Harvey and Gary, the two oldest children, had moved in during the winter and, for the first time in years, all eleven of Creola's children were living under her roof.

The Alston house on Twelfth Street had become almost a second home for many of the neighborhood youngsters—partly because Martha and Bernice had grown into attractive young ladies, and partly, I am sure, because Creola is that rare woman whose home always will be a haven for neighborhood youngsters.

Financially, too, the Alstons were better off than they ever had been previously, because Wash took on a second job in August of 1970. He left home at eight o'clock in the morning to work an eight-hour shift at the motel and returned home about five o'clock for food and several hours of sleep before leaving again to work an eight-hour night shift at an incinerator in Alexandria. Thus, he got three to four hours' sleep out of every twenty-four. But his days off were spaced so that he could rest twice a week. He worked six nights at the incinerator, with Sunday nights off; and five days at the motel, with Wednesdays and Thursdays off. At first, Creola worried about whether he could manage both jobs and keep up his health. But as the weeks passed, Wash settled into the routine and assured Creola that he would quit one job or the other if he ever began to feel that he could not manage both. When I visited them last, Wash had no plans to give up either job.

Although she was still worried about the amount of work Wash had taken on, Creola could not help being pleased about the second job because it allowed them a luxury that she had never dreamed possible—a family health-insurance plan as a fringe benefit. For the first time in her life, she could see a doctor without worrying about how to pay the bill or whether it would be paid at all. For the first time ever, her children could see a doctor any time they got sick.

Creola was also near the fulfillment of another dream when I visited them. She had started going to a dentist in August; by early October, all of her upper teeth had been removed and the gum had healed. She expected to have a full upper plate and a partial lower plate within a month.

The family cut its ties with the South when Wash let the farm go to his brother in Massachusetts; so when Wash and Creola went back to Mayflower for the Saint Stephen Homecoming Services in August of 1970, they truly went as visitors.

She enjoyed the fellowship with old friends but

found that she did not miss it as much as she might have. "If I had to go back, I could do it with joy," she told me. "But unless something happens, I really don't want to go back."

Donnie Gibson lived with his parents in South Carolina until November of 1969, growing increasingly listless as his money and prospects of a decent job diminished. He retraced his earlier round of job-hunting and listened again and again to the same answer: "We'll let you know." But they did not let him know. In October, he bought a guitar and a self-instruction manual and began to sit home for hours every day, plucking at the strings. The week before Thanksgiving, he called his brother Archie in Brooklyn and borrowed enough money to buy a ticket North. When the money came, he boarded the Chickenbone Special again, this time more willingly and more determined to stay in Brooklyn.

When I visited with him and his sisters in Brooklyn, I was left with the strong feeling that Donnie was existing in a kind of emotional limbo. He was living then in a spare, rather drab one-room apartment one door down the hall from Geraldine's apartment. He had recently been promoted to assistant foreman at the Industrial Home for the Blind, where he went to work with Archie soon after arriving in Brooklyn. He seemed rather proud of his ability to work with the handicapped, a job that called for particular patience and understanding. But I could not pull out of him any other reaction to his life beyond a bare recital of information —not because he was uncooperative, but, rather, because he seemed incapable of rising to any level of emotion or enthusiasm. Geraldine told me as much about Donnie's life in Brooklyn as Donnie did, himself.

When he arrived the second time, Donnie talked for a while about going to a trade school. (Renea's husband had given up one of his jobs and enrolled in a school, learning the air-conditioning and refrigeration trade from 9:00 A.M. to 3:00 P.M., then working a regular eight-hour shift after that.) All of his brothers and sisters wanted Donnie to enter school also, and they offered to help him financially. But Donnie could not bring himself to do it, and after several months he refused to talk about it any more. The draft appeared to be no longer a threat—although Donnie was not sure why—and his mother had long ago talked him out of joining the Navy. His life, in the fall of 1970, seemed to be a rather aimless rut of going to work and coming home. He rarely dated girls. ("Every time I meet one," he told me, "she wants to talk marriage.") Sometimes he would play basketball in the park near Public School Eleven. Mostly, he came home only to sit for hours watching television in Geraldine's apartment or, when she became irritable with him, to retreat to his guitar behind the locked door of his little apartment.

Through his mother, Donnie learned in the spring of 1970 that a part-time job was available in South Carolina—the result of one of his interviews. But he remembered the feeling of not having money in his pocket. He considered the eighty dollars a week he was bringing home in Brooklyn and decided to stay. Otis had improved sufficiently to speak on the telephone, but Donnie talked with him only occasionally.

"I don't call him as often as I used to," he told me. "I guess he figures I've forgotten him now."

The Fantastic Four had their first real reunion during the Labor Day weekend of 1970. Amos was home on leave from the Army. He had been drafted in March, and, having completed basic training and a technical school, he came home on leave before shipping out to Germany to become an electrician with the Third Infantry Division. Ernest, James and Willie came down from Rochester, where they live together and work at the same plant.

When I first met Amos, we spent a great deal of time sitting in the shade of a huge tree at the intersection where the secondary road crosses the main road to Kingstree. Amos selected the spot, and I came to suspect that it was one of his favorite places. During his twenty-one-day leave, his mother told me, Amos dated some until his three friends came down from Rochester. While they were there, she said, the four of them met every day under the tree at the crossroads. They would sit there for hours, just talking.

I never saw Georgia Mae Perry again after she left Warren County. Immediately after the graduation exercises at her high school, I left for Williamsburg County, S.C., planning to return to Warren County to travel North with her. She already had left when I got back, and her family did not know where she was. On subsequent visits North that summer and into the fall, I tried to find her in Brooklyn, Harlem, Washington and Baltimore. Once, I thought I had located her. I found a

Georgia M. Perry who worked in a gift shop in a Baltimore suburb; I walked into the shop about closing time one night, feeling the way some ancient quester might if he were about to touch the Holy Grail. When Miss Perry at the gift shop turned out to be an elderly lady who had lived in Baltimore for forty years, I gave up the search.

Wherever she is, I hope that Georgia Mae—like the others in this story—has found a productive place in society for herself.